RUSTIC *Joyful* FOOD

RUSTIC *Joyful* FOOD

Generations

DANIELLE KARTES

Photography by Jeff Hobson & Michael Kartes

Copyright © 2017, 2020 by Danielle Kartes
Cover and internal design © 2020 by Sourcebooks
Cover design by Brittany Vibbert
Cover and internal images © Michael Kartes
Internal design by Jillian Rahn
Food and prop styling by Danielle Kartes

Sourcebooks and the colophon are registered trademarks of Sourcebooks.

All rights reserved. No part of this book may be reproduced in any form or by any electronic or mechanical means including information storage and retrieval systems—except in the case of brief quotations embodied in critical articles or reviews—without permission in writing from its publisher, Sourcebooks.

This publication is designed to provide accurate and authoritative information in regard to the subject matter covered. It is sold with the understanding that the publisher is not engaged in rendering legal, accounting, or other professional service. If legal advice or other expert assistance is required, the services of a competent professional person should be sought. —*From a Declaration of Principles Jointly Adopted by a Committee of the American Bar Association and a Committee of Publishers and Associations*

All brand names and product names used in this book are trademarks, registered trademarks, or trade names of their respective holders. Sourcebooks is not associated with any product or vendor in this book.

Published by Sourcebooks
P.O. Box 4410, Naperville, Illinois 60567-4410
(630) 961-3900
sourcebooks.com

Originally published in 2017 in the United States by Lavender Press.

Library of Congress Cataloging-in-Publication Data

Names: Kartes, Danielle, author. | Kartes, Michael, photographer.
Title: Rustic joyful food : generations / Danielle Kartes ; photography by
   Michael Kartes.
Description: Naperville, Illinois : Sourcebooks, 2020. | Includes index.
Identifiers: LCCN 2019025316 | (hardcover)
Subjects: LCSH: Comfort food. | LCGFT: Cookbooks.
Classification: LCC TX714 .K3676 2020 | DDC 641.3--dc23
LC record available at https://lccn.loc.gov/2019025316

Printed and bound in China.
OGP 10 9 8 7 6 5 4 3 2 1

Recipe for Watergate C[ake]

1 Box white cake mix
1 Box instant pistachio pudding
1 C Salad Oil
1 C Club soda
3 eggs and ½ c chopped nuts

Mix in order given. Bake at 350°
for 40 minutes in 9 X 13 greased pan

Topping

1 Box instant pistachio pudding

---

7 rozen Lemo[n]
combine 2 egg yolks,
pint whipping ⅓ cup cup
cream 2 tbsp. lemon
½ tsp. grated
Cook in double boiler
about 3 min. stir consta[ntly]
Beat 2 egg whites until
2 tbsp. sugar gradually
fold whites into lem[on]
fold in ⅔ cup (or 1 cup [of]

¼ tsp. salt
1 tsp. soda
5 heaping tsp. [cocoa]
1 tsp. vanilla

---

1 cup sugar
1¾ cup flour

Beat cream & eggs together. Add flour,
salt, soda and cocoa. Beat Thoroughly.
vanilla. Bake in two layer pans - grease[d]

---

pan, add molasses and
add flour, salt, baking soda a[nd]
g. chill. Shape into b[alls]
Bake @ 325° for
balls 20 min. makes 4 a[?]

Marina[ted?]
3H Carrots
Clean - Cu[t]

Date Oatmeal Cookies   350°

cook slowly until thick:
1 cup pitted, chopped dates
½ cup sugar
½ cup water

Cream together: ½ cup shortening, ½ cup
brown sugar - then add 1½ cup flour,
¼ tsp. baking soda, ½ tsp salt. Add 1¼

Peanut Butter Cookies

For Milo and Noah
Ephesians 3:20

God can do anything, you know—far more than you could ever imagine or guess or request in your wildest dreams!

For My Grandmother Gloria

Your life is a gift.
Psalm 78:3–4

Things we have heard and known, things our ancestors have told us. We will tell the next generation the praiseworthy deeds of the Lord, His power, and the wonders He has done.

For My Brother William (The Baby)

We've come a long way since the lemon bars.

To Every Mother

To every mother up all night, eating the bits off your kids' plates and longing for a hot shower: You are brave. You made a tiny human, or several. You are creating a legacy.

To every mother flying out the door to work with dry toast in one hand and backpacks in the other: Fret not; you are doing a good job.

To every woman with a child who doubts her abilities and is doing the very best she can: Take heart, for you are creating a generation. Your love won't ever go unnoticed, and your shortcomings will be forgiven.

I've heard it said that the days are long and the years are short. Revel in these years. These are your training years. You are being refined and tried and tested for a purpose. Motherhood is messy and unscripted, and you will fail, but you will soar. Embrace your flaws, and forgive yourself. Those tiny people want only you—your love and your time. They don't want perfect, and they don't need pretty; they just need you. Cook them all the food from scratch that you can manage. They won't forget. Play with them, and hold them always, no matter what the books say. They want the real you.

To every mother: You've got this. You were made for hard things.

Contents

— ◆◇◆ —

Introduction   xvii

Measurements   xxv

Supper   1

Stuffed Shells   5
Fresh Pasta with Tiger Shrimp and Cream   6
Oven-Baked BBQ Chicken Wings   7
Curried Halibut   9
Cafeteria Chicken Gravy   10
Gloria's Oven-Fried Chicken Legs   12
The Ultimate Classic Beer-Battered Fish and Chips   15
Puff Pastry Roast Beef Pot Pie   17
Wine-and-Tomato-Braised Short Ribs over Parmesan
   Cauliflower Mash   19

My Mom's Swiss Steak	20
Mustard Chicken Thighs and Cauliflower	21
Old-School Cracker Crumb Nuggets and Sauces	23
Seared Salmon with Citronette-Dressed Greens	25
Homemade Sheet-Pan Pizza	26
Homestyle Meatloaf Sandwich	29
Apple Cider Pork Shoulder with Thyme and Sauerkraut	30
Angel Hair Pasta in Tomato Cream	31
Swedish-Style Meatballs in Mushroom Cream Sauce	33
Turkey Gravy	34
Shepherd's Pie	35
Stovetop Mac 'n' Cheese	37
Smothered Chicken and Mushroom Gravy	38
Garlic Butter Shrimp	40
Fresh Crab Feast	40
Toasted Pimento Cheese Sandwiches	42
Sheet-Pan Chicken and Carrots	43
Sloppy Joes	44
Mustard-Roasted Chicken and Potatoes	46
Company Chicken	47
Baked Chicken Parmesan	49
Olive Chicken	51

Soups and Stews 55

Bacon and White Bean Soup	57
Hamburger Soup	58
Real Baked Potato Soup	59
Bouillabaisse or Fish Stew	61
Classic Oven-Braised Beef and Tomato Stew over Cream Cheese Polenta	63
Potato, Parsnip, and Celeriac Root Vegetable Soup	64
Curried Carrot Soup	67
Perfect Chicken Stock	69
Classic New England Clam Chowder Bread Bowls	71
Taco Soup	72
Roasted Tomato Soup	75
Thai Green Curry Soup with Grilled Chicken Skewers	76

Vegetables and Sides 79

Herby Peas	83
Creamy Buttermilk and Parsley Mashed Potatoes	84
Butternut Squash Polenta	85
Creamed Spinach	85
Aunty Pat's Dilly Potatoes	86
Roasted Carrots with Cilantro Yogurt	89
Garlic and Brown Butter Asparagus	90
Roasted Butternut Squash with Parmesan Cheese	91
Easter Potatoes with Feta, Cream Cheese, and Dill	92
Roasted Cauliflower and Capers	95
Off-the-Cob Street Corn with Chipotle and Feta	97

Kale and Fresh Crab Caesar Salad with Pepita Caesar Dressing	98
Peas and Orzo	101
Everyday Green Salad	103
Thora's Steakhouse Crispy Onion Rings with Buttermilk Ranch Dipping Sauce	104
Tomato and Cucumber Salad	106
Cream Cheese Polenta	107
Roasted Radishes	109
Spring Potatoes	109
Jenny's Perfectly Steamed Broccoli and Cauliflower	110
Mom's Scalloped Potatoes	111
Old-Fashioned Dill and Mustard Potato Salad	113
Roasted Winter Vegetables	114

Snacks 117

White Cheddar Toast with Dill and Tomatoes	121
Homestyle Garlic Fries	123
Pickles	125
Rosemary and Parmesan Popcorn	126
Spicy Sweet Potato Fries with Sun-Dried Tomato Mayo	127
Buttermilk Fried Oysters and Razor Clams	129
Caramelized Brie and Tomatoes	131

Breakfast 133

Cinnamon Vanilla Ricotta Pancakes	136
Blueberry Brown Sugar Baked French Toast Topped with Toasted Pecans, Buttermilk Maple Syrup, and Whipped Cream	138
Caramelized Onion Frittata	141
Sweet Potato Hash and Fried Eggs	142
Whole-Grain Waffles with Apple Butterscotch Syrup	143
Buttermilk Pumpkin Pancakes with Toasted Pecans and Cream Cheese Schmear	144
Fluffy Cornbread and Maple Syrup	147
Soft Scrambled Eggs	148
Chocolate Chip and Rye Pancakes	149
Bus-Stop Egg Sandwiches	151
Yogurt Bowls with Stewed Apples	155
Baked Chiles Rellenos	156
Cream of Wheat	157

Drinks 159

Old-Fashioned Lemonade	161
Grapefruit Paloma	161
Hot Chocolate	163
Cider Champagne Cocktail	163
Italian Sodas	164
Egg Coffee	167
Mojito Floats	168

Sweets 171

Aunt Libby's Carrot Cake	173
Cherry Chip Cake with Cream Cheese Icing	174
Chocolate Buttermilk Birthday Cake with Malted Chocolate Cream Cheese Frosting	175
Grandma Hawkins's Applesauce Bundt Cake	176
Cream Cheese Brownies	178
Spiced Stewed Apples	179
Dark Chocolate and Cherry Cream Cheese Whoopie Pies	181
Coconut Bundt Cake with Lemon Curd, Toasted Coconut, and Soft Whipped Cream	182
Coconut Cream Lemon Bars	185
Honey Butter Biscuit Strawberry Shortcake	187
Mug Cakes, a.k.a. the Emotional Support Treat	191
Molasses and Walnut Zucchini Bread	192
Pineapple and Cherry Crumble	194
Cream Cheese and Honey Fruit Dip	194
Walnut Pie	195
Pumpkin Yogurt Snack Cake	196
Cinnamon and Sugar Toasts	197
Peanut Butter and Jam Cookie Bars	199
Salted Caramel Apples	200
Weeknight Yellow Cake with Fudge Frosting	202
Spiced Pumpkin Scones with Spiced Cream Icing	203
Vanilla Bean Sugar Cookies	205
Sticky Toffee Pudding	208
White Cake with Raspberry Jam and Coconut	210
Dark Chocolate and Salted Caramel Panna Cotta	213
Lemon Chiffon Pie	214
Old-Fashioned Rice Pudding	215

Strawberry Galette with Crème Fraîche	216
Fresh Blueberry and Chocolate Chip Cookies	219
Apricot and Almond Shortbread Galette	220
Pear and Almond Cream Tart	222

Closing Thoughts 225

Index 227

About the Author 237

Introduction

Generations—good food, warm sun, humble beginnings, and a whole lot of faith

I grew up on Kool-Aid, butter-flavored Crisco, and homemade bread! It warms me to recall those long-ago summers: standing on a chair and dumping sugar into a lidless plastic pitcher, swirling the sugar and powder until ribbons of colored juice appeared, sipping from the spoon I stirred it with, pouring cups for my brothers and sister, then flying out the back sliding-glass door to play again. It wasn't what we were drinking that makes my childhood memories special; it was the carefree feeling of being part of a family and all that comes with it: learning and growing together, never perfect but always loving.

I have long since abandoned my Kool-Aid ways and now opt to cook with organic and wholesome food whenever possible, but that doesn't mean we don't splurge and have a little fun every now and again.

What makes a meal special? Certainly not the best cutlery, the most expensive ingredients, or the latest trends in cooking. We don't necessarily remember foods for their expense or extravagance, but for the memories they evoke. It's about the people who made them for you and how they loved you. I have always known there was something special about Grandma Gloria's oven-fried chicken, and I knew that the pains of life were somehow healed in the kitchen. There is this beautiful tradition in families, no matter what yours looks like. It does not matter *what* is served but *how* it's served. There are stories and cultures and ways of life that have been forgotten, but certain things will always remain.

Generations past worked for us to have better. As a kid, during lean times, there was such a sense of victory when enough change was gathered to buy a gallon of milk. I can remember how I always thought my mom was the most beautiful mom out there. I was privy

As the generations move on, you not only feel but see the fingerprints, in your everyday life and in your home, of those who've passed on.

to much as a child, but it's not until now, having my own children, that I fully understand the effort made by my mother to keep our family comfortable during times of financial hardship and how she valiantly weathered those times for us kids. There was always food on our table, and it was always delicious. We had a garden every year. My dad worked two jobs for most of my childhood. He served in the army for thirty-eight years, active and reserve, put himself through night school, and worked in education. He'd come home from teaching all day, and we'd have dinner waiting for him to take to the penitentiary, where he taught life skills to prisoners, some of whom were even on death row.

Fresh-baked cookies, hearty soups, and hunks of fresh bread—family food—were always in our home. We ate dinner early, around four o'clock, so Dad could get a hot meal on the way to his second full-time job. His actions and dedication to our family are what shaped me into who I am. When you don't have all the money in the world and you do have a big family, using everything is essential to life.

Hamburger patties, home fries and corn, spaghetti and garlic bread, pot roast. Throw in some fish sticks and baked chicken, yellow cake on a weeknight for no good reason—these were our staples. Homemade wasn't trendy when I was a child; it was just life. We had hamburger soup (as we liked to call it) at least once a week: rich vegetable broth and loads of ground chuck, potatoes, carrots, tomatoes, and any other veggie that happened to be in the crisper. There were chicken thighs braised in homemade barbecue sauce for hours, which we'd eat with white rice. These unfancy, flavorful dishes are what I make for my own family, along with new favorites.

I learned from my mother not just to cook but to feed people. When we were small, she'd make big pots of soup for the homeless shelter. I wasn't even tall enough to see into the pot, but I knew the food she was making was going to feed those who had nothing, even when we had very little. You always give, and you always try.

My mother learned to cook from her grandmother, my great-gran Thora. Thora Pederson grew up on a farm in North Dakota in the 1920s. Born in 1917, she was the youngest of ten. Her family sold milk and cream, butter and wheat. Their farm was simple, and times were lean. They worked tirelessly to eat. She has long since gone to be with Jesus, and as I write, I wish she had known that how she grew up and lived would speak to my life now, some eighty years later. My great-grandmother cooked with all the gusto and fortitude of a Norwegian nana who grew up in the Dakotas: butter, gravy, and apple pie.

Thora got a job when she was twelve and moved into the city to care for some children as a nanny. She went to high school for two years, until her family needed her to quit and work to send money home to the farm. When she was just seventeen, she met a man twenty years her senior, and they married. They moved from North Dakota to Montana, then to Oregon to follow the work. Their family often ate rice pudding. She started her career in the food industry by chance, as a dishwasher, in the '50s. Then she worked her way up the line into salads. She created the dressing and onion-ring recipes still used to this day at a popular steakhouse. She continued to move up and work hard and soon owned a cafeteria in an Oregon Sears building. All eight of her kids worked there, and the food was all-American and heavenly, including the mustard and dill potato salad we still eat to this day—the same potato salad Great-Gran made to feed a tiny crowd on my mother's wedding day in 1980. The wedding feast was ham, baked beans, and that same classic potato salad, with punch, coffee service, and white cake for dessert. What I wouldn't give to have cooked alongside her.

Gresham, Oregon. Auntie Ingrid and Uncle Telvin's dairy farm.

My grandmother Gloria was the eldest of Great-Gran's eight children. Gloria, when she had a family of her own in the '60s, was the new American woman. She spent twelve-to-fourteen-hour days outside the home, doing factory work, so her young family would not go hungry. She made a few things for my mom that were a real treat, like oven-fried chicken and relish trays for entertaining, with pickles and sliced tomatoes, and chocolate cupcakes with white icing. My mother inherited tenacity from her mother and a soul for cooking from her grandmother.

I believe my adoration and need to cook came from these

Duarte, California. My dad, Michael, and his beloved Grandma Mac (MacLoughlin).

deep roots. When I opened my restaurant, it became a place to practice everything I'd learned in my life and was a source of creativity, love, and real joy.

As the generations move on, you not only feel but see the fingerprints, in your everyday life and in your home, of those who've passed on. I get a sense of who they were at mealtimes: unspoken tradition, fixing a plate the way your mother did, the way my mother did.

I believe there is a food renaissance beginning. People are taking great care in cooking again, figuring out how to eat better and figuring out how to get back to those days of slow-cooked, homegrown food while balancing a career and family. I've been part of a revolution and a connection to the past while always pushing forward.

When my sons were born, motherhood took on an entirely different meaning for me. It's been my job to love and teach these curious children about how I was raised and about the mistakes I've made. I believe that they're going to live their lives better than those who've gone before them. My boys are my gift. Noah is my right-hand man in the kitchen, and at just six years old, he can roll fresh pasta and scramble eggs with the best of 'em. We go on trips to the city to watch how things are made, and his love for cooking and life is deeply rooted in the generations that came before him; for this I am grateful. When I think of generations past, I am grateful. Because of their struggle, we are afforded an easier way of life.

When I first met my husband, he said something so profound when I asked him his favorite color: "The sunlight in the photographs from my childhood." This nostalgic sentiment is relatable, no matter who you are, and it especially applies to the food we ate growing up. Ramen noodles might trigger late-night studying memories, or chili mac and steamed broccoli might remind you of busy school nights—that go-to meal your family loves that you can have on the table in twenty minutes.

The recipes in this book are simple and delicious. These are the foods I grew up on and the foods I now feed my family. They are meant to remind you how special family time is and how important memories made around food truly are.

This book—it's who I am. It's who we all are: messy and happy and filled with joy and sometimes regret. Filled with hope and love and promise that there will always be good in the world. *Rustic Joyful Food* is about life, and *Generations* is about the past that will always touch our present and continue to shape our future.

The smell of cinnamon transports you back to your childhood, fulfilling your longing for a sweeter time. Not because the present isn't good, but because the good old days filled with life and hardship and buttermilk biscuits and smothered chicken seemed to make you just a little bit of you are.

We had backyard chickens in the suburbs.

My family did everything we could to experience every season. Berry picking and making jam seem so trendy these days, but it was a way of life for us—foraging and picking. We were poor and happy. We enjoyed free lunch at public school. I never knew we were any different from any other family.

Our Hawkins tribe took the seasons seriously, and we pushed the limits. When it snowed, we sneaked into vacant houses' backyards to go sledding in mixing bowls. I'd sell water in big 7-Eleven cups to construction workers while they replaced our streets.

I was a different kid. I was raised with a voice. My parents taught me to question authority and follow my gut. I had a full-blown candy business out of my eighth-grade backpack. I was taught to make something out of nothing, and somehow my mom could always manage to rub two nickels together and make food that rivaled all foods. We were poor and so richly blessed. Never once was a limit ever placed on achieving our dreams or goals. Dreaming was a part of life. Drive was passed out freely in our house. My dad always said, "Poor doesn't equal dirty," and my mother took great care in us.

This is a book about home. About where we are shaped. About

This is a book about home. About where we are shaped. About the food that is passed down.

I learned from my mother not just to cook but to feed people.

the food that is passed down. It's a raw look at family life, no matter what yours might look like. It's about immigration and farm life in the '20s, and it's about grit and virtue. It's about Jesus and egg coffees. Lemon chiffon pies and my heritage. That ache to touch just a part of it as an adult and savor every damn moment in life. God gives us this one go-round, and it'd better be your best attempt. Never perfect, but always trying to be better for my own babies. For my husband, for myself.

There are characters in my story who might be just like yours, and they might breathe life into your heart by reading about them. There is pain in life, and somehow it seems to me it'll be healed by food: nourishing our souls and living for the Lord because time isn't promised.

This summer, we welcomed our sweet boy Milo into our family (Milo means "merciful").

God was so very merciful to bless us with this tiny lion heart, a true fighter. Milo was born eight weeks prematurely; he fought for his life valiantly, and God granted it to him. My pregnancy wasn't easy. Living through this summer in the hospital, battling for our family and warring for my tiny human, taught me so much. It humbled me to be in the NICU with this baby for five weeks, and it humbled me to be in the ICU myself with so many complications in my own healing. One evening, while I could barely eat, sixty miles from my three-pound newborn in another hospital in another city, my sister came into my room with a small container of home-cooked food.

I had been lying in a hospital bed the better part of a month, and this time it was much more serious. My sister had some pot roast and mashed potatoes. Nothing in the world tasted as good as that home-cooked food. I cried while I ate it.

God had given me a phrase for our family at the beginning of 2017. He gently whispered to my soul: *Move forward.* I had little idea what that meant. Reflecting ten weeks after Milo was born, I understood what He meant: *Just take each day a step at a time. Move forward just a little each morning. Press on.*

That food my sissy brought me gave me just what I needed to press on a little more. Food heals. We continue to move forward in our journey and in our healing and in life. I savor each moment. I

Washington State. Dad and me.

love my boys so fiercely, and I am grateful to do life with my very best friend. He brings out the fire in me, and I love him for it. To think God trusted us with these two boys is a wild gift. They are my legacy.

They represent generations to come, and they hold just a piece of the past.

I'm a cook who learned to cook from my mom and developed my style for messy, simple, happy recipes in the last ten years, cooking in my own restaurant and gleaning every bit of knowledge I could from other chefs and colleagues. I want you to share in my life and enjoy these recipes, to make them your own.

My husband likes to tell me I'm one of the rare ones who never signed the unspoken social contract. I love that description of me: out here breaking rules and blazing trails and inviting others to come along for the ride and blaze their own paths.

Measurements

I have never seen any grandmother use a set of measuring cups. All growing up, my mom would grab a large metal bowl and just begin to dump in ingredients using no form of measurement, let alone scale, and she'd come up with cookies that rivaled all cookies, or tender crumb banana bread that had all the nooks and crannies to hold a pat of butter.

When I first moved out, I wanted that same skill set. I tried dumping ingredients into a bowl and mixing them up, but my baked goods always tasted like leather, my cookies like hockey pucks. Banana bread? Flat and lifeless. I needed to be a seasoned cook before I knew the way something looked or felt. I just wanted to be the best without the trials. Now, after fifteen years of solid cooking, I understand the chemistry behind baking more than I did as a kid. I've lived through the preparation of so many dishes. I understand each ingredient's role in a cake or stew. More isn't always better; restraint in cooking is an art form. I look at cooking as this dance. I didn't know that browning meat made the difference in layering flavors or that overworking your dough yields a tough end result.

Life produces a great cook. Not school, not all the best ingredients. Hard times breed creativity. Rent week leads me to cook things in such a way that even a can of beans sings.

Necessity is the mother of invention, and time heals all kitchen-related wounds. Even for the worst cook. Success is a habit formed by failing and then trying again. Honestly, I can now make a batch of chocolate chip cookies to rival all chocolate chip cookies by dumping a bunch of ingredients into a bowl and adding the one extra ingredient it took me a long time to understand how to use: experience.

My experiences in life have really shown me how to cook, how to incorporate love into everything I make, and how to fail with grace. Cooking with love is this grand journey. I've never been interested in learning to cook perfectly. I've never desired to slice a perfect chiffonade or slice carrots into impressive julienne sticks. These things are impressive and special to many people, but for me, what's special is heart and soul. Soul injected into the food I cook is far more important than the techniques of folks who wears chef's hats. "Yes, chef!" in the kitchen doesn't sound as pure as "Wow, how can I make something so delicious for my family?" There is no ego in home cooking. It's not the best of the best.

Or is it? For me, the answer is, and always will be, yes. The bits and pieces and odds and ends that make up the family meal are indeed the very best of the best. Braising and roasting and sautéing seasonal, affordable food is my very favorite way to cook. I am a cook; I am not a chef. I like it this way. I've learned to measure by life's hand, and I wouldn't have it any other way. To feed you is to truly love you. I will continue to feed and to feel the way a dish needs to be, all while showing the world that there is value in the in-between. The in-between is where life happens.

> An item of note in regard to the recipes in this book:
> *Always use 1 teaspoon of kosher salt per pound of meat. All meats.*

Supper

An Ode to Supper at 4:00 p.m.

Flopped on the couch, covered in black grime and a cutoff black sweatshirt, was a very tired father. My dad lost his job when I was about ten, and our whole world changed. I remember it being difficult in all the expected ways. But he kept on going. He got multiple odd jobs and kept working hard, always. He didn't take this setback as an excuse to feel sorry for himself. He began working his way through night school. He never stopped. I see these snippets of him when I close my eyes, memories of him just *doing*.

He liked to unwind by hanging out in the garage, listening to classical music as he sorted baseball cards late into the night, or sorting ammo or military gear. I remember him covered in oil and grime from working on the pickup—that old Ford always needed something. It had no power steering for much of my childhood, among other shortcomings. Is there anything sweeter than seeing your dad fix *everything*?

All the while, he stayed in the army reserves, working his way up to sergeant major, the highest rank for an enlisted soldier. He eventually got his bachelor's degree, then went on to earn his master's degree and teaching and administration credentials. He got a job at a small private school. His philosophy has always been that you can turn any situation into what you want it to be, what you've dreamed of. You can always find a way to be what you are called to be. Your station in life is determined by you and no one else.

He always said, "Poor doesn't equal dirty, so take care of your things." I inherited his cluttered nature and his drive. I began attending the private high school where he worked when I was a sophomore, and I hated it. I didn't know it at the time, but attending that school, where I didn't fit in and I wasn't like most of the other kids, was honestly the best thing for me. I learned to really love who I was. What a treasure to go to school where my dad taught. I'd get to hang out in his classroom, observing how all my fellow students just loved him. They loved that he was invested in them, that he saw all they could be. My dad loved the "labeled" kids—the sad kids, the kids who some might say didn't have a bright future. He saw those kids, mentored those kids, and changed those kids' lives. And he does so to this day.

When we'd head to school in the winter, I wasn't embarrassed by our lack of cool stuff in a school filled with privileged kids. I was always proud that we wrapped up in old blankets and piled into the pickup with no power steering or a heater to go to school. My siblings and I would crack up and give Dad plenty of room to take the turns nice and early. He'd start cranking that wheel *long before* we reached the turn!

Even when he was teaching, my dad worked multiple jobs to provide for his family and their future. Five nights a week after school, he'd have just enough time to grab dinner and run out the door to his second teaching job. My mom would fix a hearty dinner (eating out was a rare luxury for us), making all the foods found in this chapter. Dinner had to be ready by 4:00 p.m. sharp, much earlier than my friends' families ate. She'd fix big pots of soup or meatloaf or pasta. Some days, Dad would pull his chair up to the table and eat, then my mom would pack up a sandwich or an additional portion of food for him to take along when he left.

He'd head out to the prison where he taught life skills to prisoners in isolation. Through a thick pane of glass, he taught men on death row how to read and write. I was so curious about my father's jobs. I'd ask what crimes the men he taught had committed, and he'd say, "Don't know, don't care." I didn't realize what an incredible statement that was when I was young. He truly didn't care; he saw all they *could* be instead of what they were. He saw broken people who needed to be believed in.

One day, my dad sold that old pickup to help pay the bills. Now, every so often, I'll see an old cream-colored Ford pickup from the seventies and think of everything that truck taught me through my dad. Dinner at 4:00 p.m. is important; it means you're gettin' stuff done.

To this day, my own family eats early; that way, it leaves plenty of time for seconds and a bedtime snack of cake for no good reason other than it's fun and we can. When I think of my dad, I think of dinner at 4:00 p.m. and peach pie and banana pudding. I think of motor oil and off-the-cuff one-liners. I think of endless hard work and bringing yourself up no matter what your circumstances look like. I think of how humble he is and how he doesn't want any attention. I think of saltine crackers and butter or hot dogs chopped up into cans of beans. Because of my dad, I'll forever treasure supper at 4:00 p.m.

PREP TIME: 45 minutes COOK TIME: 35–40 minutes
YIELD: 4–6 servings

Stuffed Shells

INGREDIENTS

1 pound dried jumbo pasta
shells (manicotti shells are a
wonderful substitute)

SAUCE

1 (28-ounce) can your favorite
crushed tomatoes

4 fresh tomatoes, sliced

1 large yellow onion, sliced

½ cup butter

½ cup chopped fresh basil

Salt and pepper to taste

FILLING

1 pound ground turkey

1 pound Italian sausage

1 large yellow onion, diced

¼ cup chopped fresh basil

1 cup shredded parmesan
cheese

1 (15-ounce) container whole
milk ricotta

2 cloves fresh garlic, crushed

Salt and pepper to taste

2 cups shredded mozzarella
cheese

DIRECTIONS

Boil the noodles according to the package directions and set
aside. Combine all sauce ingredients in a large pot, and simmer
over medium heat for 45 minutes.

Brown the turkey, sausage, and onion in a separate pan over
medium-high heat until onion is caramelized. The deeper the
color, the better the filling will taste. Put the mixture in a large
mixing bowl and add the rest of the filling ingredients. It's
okay that it's hot. Be sure to continue checking and stirring
your sauce.

Once the filling is prepped and the sauce is done, preheat the
oven to 350°, then set up an assembly line. Put all the sauce in a
9-by-13-inch baking dish or skillet, and begin to stuff your pasta
shells. Depending on the shell size, a large tablespoon of filling
will fit nicely. I like to overfill each shell. Nestle the stuffed pasta
into the sauce and repeat the process, tightly packing shells in
next to one another until the pan is full. You may have an excess
of filling and a few shells; layer them in a separate dish and
refrigerate for later or bake along with the others.

Bake shells for 35 to 45 minutes, until they become golden
brown, then sprinkle shredded mozzarella over top, and
continue to bake for 5 additional minutes.

SUPPER

PREP TIME: 1 hour COOK TIME: 1 hour YIELD: 4–6 servings

Fresh Pasta with Tiger Shrimp and Cream

FRESH PASTA

3–4 cups all-purpose or
  semolina flour

4–6 fresh eggs

SHRIMP AND CREAM

½ cup butter

2 tablespoons olive oil or
  citronette

1 onion, sliced

1 whole head garlic, peeled and
  chopped

2 pounds peeled and deveined
  shrimp, tails on or off

4 cups heavy cream

Salt and pepper to taste

1 cup shredded parmesan
  cheese

½ cup chopped fresh parsley

FOR THE PASTA

Knead the eggs and flour by hand until smooth. This process requires patience and a good feel for the dough. The entire process should take about 20 minutes. Use the heel of your hand to work the dough to the proper consistency; it will feel like you might have done something wrong, but keep going. Add flour if the dough is too sticky and an egg if it's too dry. When the dough is smooth and soft, cover it in plastic wrap, and let it rest in the fridge for at least 30 minutes.

Roll the pasta out according to your machine requirements, keeping each layer floured and separated. Boil a large pot of salted water, and cook pasta gently for 2 to 3 minutes; set aside in a strainer until ready to add to the cream sauce.

FOR THE CREAM SAUCE

Melt the butter and oil in a 12-inch skillet over medium heat. Sauté the onion and garlic in the butter and oil until soft. Add shrimp, cook until just done, then remove from the skillet. Add the cream, salt, and pepper, and cook 2 to 3 minutes, or until the cream begins to bubble, scraping the bottom of the skillet with a wooden spoon.

Add the cooked pasta, and gently fold it into the cream. If the cream feels tight, add a ladle of pasta-cooking water. Add cheese, parsley, and shrimp to the pan, and gently fold to combine. Taste for seasoning, and enjoy!

PREP TIME: 5 minutes COOK TIME: 90 minutes YIELD: 4 servings

Oven-Baked BBQ Chicken Wings

Homemade BBQ sauce was the very first thing I remember cooking as a kid. I loved to basically take all the condiments on the side door of the refrigerator and make something so delicious. We always ate an early dinner because my dad worked two jobs, and when he got home from one job, my mom would have dinner waiting by 4:00 p.m. so he could be out the door to his second full-time job. This meal is so wonderful: you basically dump sauce on the wings and bake them until they are fall-apart tender and caramelized.

INGREDIENTS

3 pounds chicken wings

½ cup chopped green onions

½ cup chopped fresh parsley
   (reserve a handful for the end)

½ cup ketchup

½ cup soy sauce or tamari

¼ cup vinegar, any kind

2 tablespoons brown sugar

2 tablespoons mustard

2 tablespoons olive oil

1 tablespoon tomato paste

2 cloves fresh garlic, crushed

Salt and pepper to taste

DIRECTIONS

Preheat the oven to 350°. Lay wings in a 9-by-13-inch baking dish. Whisk together all sauce ingredients, and pour over the wings.

Cover tightly with foil, and bake covered for 60 minutes and uncovered for 30 minutes.

Serve with rice or quinoa. Spoon the sauce over rice; it's wonderful. Sprinkle fresh, chopped herbs over the dish to finish.

SUPPER 7

Curried Halibut

PREP TIME: 20 minutes COOK TIME: 20 minutes YIELD: 4 servings

Curried Halibut

My dad went halibut fishing this summer and brought back some of the tastiest fish I'd ever had. We prepared the halibut in countless ways, including grilling it and sautéing it in garlic butter. This meaty, flaky, tender fish is lovely no matter how you prepare it. It's warm, creative, loaded with flavor, and absolutely comforting. The fish poaches gently in under 7 minutes in the curry, and the entire thing comes together in 30 minutes.

INGREDIENTS

1 yellow onion, sliced

1 pinch crushed red pepper flakes

2 tablespoons olive oil

2 tablespoons curry paste (your preference is fine; I use a mild Indian red curry)

3 cloves fresh garlic, smashed

1 medium zucchini, sliced

2 cups chopped fresh tomatoes

Salt and pepper to taste

1 cup chicken stock

1 (15-ounce) can full-fat coconut milk

1 pound fresh halibut or meaty whitefish, cut into 2-inch cubes

Lime and chopped cilantro for garnish (optional)

DIRECTIONS

Preheat a large, nonstick sauté pan over medium heat. Sauté the onion and pepper flakes in olive oil with the curry paste until onions are translucent, about 5 minutes. Add garlic; sauté for another minute. Add vegetables and salt and pepper to taste.

Cook the veggies until tender, and add chicken stock and coconut milk. Reduce heat to low, and simmer 20 to 30 minutes, uncovered.

Lightly season the fish with salt and pepper, and gently place each piece into the simmering curry to poach. Cook for 2 to 3 minutes per side, turning just once.

Remove from heat, and serve over white basmati or jasmine rice; garnish with fresh lime and cilantro.

PREP TIME: 10 minutes COOK TIME: 2½–3 hours YIELD: 4 servings

Cafeteria Chicken Gravy

When I was in elementary school, we'd get a hot-lunch calendar at the beginning of the month detailing what was to be served each day. I was about ten and in the fourth grade when I saw "Holiday Lunch Option." Nothing else was listed. Such mystery! There were four of us kids in my family, and we got to pick hot lunch once, maybe twice, a month for really special occasions. I saw Holiday Lunch Option, and I fancied myself a gambling woman. I was in! When I arrived at school, all I could think about was lunchtime. WHAT COULD IT BE? When the lunch bell rang, I flew to the front of the class and waited eagerly for dismissal. I could smell something delicious as we rounded the corner of the library in a perfect line of twenty-four kids, converging with other classes, all of us filtering into the lunch hall. I grabbed my tray and placed it on the counter. Plop—mashed potatoes; this was promising! Then came the gravy with little bits of chicken meat. This was right up my alley. I was so impressed! I'd had gravy and potatoes many times but never with the chicken mixed into the gravy! I laugh when I think back to that day and remember my excitement. Little did I know I would tuck the memory away for a recipe years later. I love to make this homestyle comfort food in the fall for my boys. When my mom was going through chemotherapy, I remember her asking me to make my chicken gravy and potatoes. That might have been one of the dearest meals I have ever cooked.

CHICKEN

1 medium yellow onion, sliced

2 cups water

1 whole chicken (4–5 pounds)

2 tablespoons butter, softened

2 tablespoons kosher salt

1 tablespoon freshly cracked
 black pepper

FOR THE CHICKEN

Preheat the oven to 300°. Put the onion and water in an enamel-covered Dutch oven or oven-safe lidded pot, then put the chicken on top. Rub the entire bird with butter, then salt and pepper, taking care to get underneath the skin wherever possible.

Bake the chicken for 2½ to 3 hours, covered; chicken should be falling off the bone.

Remove the chicken to a platter for 30 minutes to cool, reserving all cooking liquids. When the chicken is cool enough to handle, remove the meat from the bones, and set aside. Save the bones and skin for perfect chicken stock.

CONTINUED

Cafeteria Chicken Gravy

GRAVY

½ cup butter

¼ cup all-purpose flour

3 cups low-sodium chicken
stock or broth

At least 3 cups reserved liquids
and onion from the chicken
baking pot

½ cup heavy cream

Salt and pepper to taste

Fresh rosemary or thyme
(optional)

FOR THE GRAVY

Melt the butter in a large saucepan, then whisk in the flour. Cook
this roux until it bubbles, at least 2 minutes, to cook off the gritty
flour taste.

Slowly whisk in the chicken stock or broth along with the
cooking liquids from the chicken. Bring to a simmer over
medium heat for about 5 minutes (steep fresh rosemary or thyme
in the gravy during this time, if desired). Gravy should thicken
but not be overly thick; you are looking for a creamy, pourable
consistency.

Add the cream and cooked shredded chicken to finish. Serve over
Creamy Buttermilk and Parsley Mashed Potatoes (see recipe on
page 84).

PREP TIME: 25 minutes COOK TIME: 90 minutes YIELD: 4–6 servings

Gloria's Oven-Fried Chicken Legs

When I was ten and loved dinnertime, there was nothing quite like my grandma Gloria's chicken legs. We'd go to her house, mostly on Sundays after church, and she'd have a relish tray (pickles, olives, and sliced tomatoes). I'm sure there were lots of other side dishes, but I didn't care about any of them. I was there for the chicken—the juicy, fall-apart, drippy chicken legs with the salty, crunchy, oily crust. These are the things dreams are made of, and I know she learned these from her mother, my great-gran Thora.

INGREDIENTS

18 chicken legs

2 cups buttermilk

Sea salt and pepper to taste

3 cups mild oil, suitable for frying

3 cups all-purpose flour

DIRECTIONS

Soak the chicken in buttermilk for at least one hour and up to overnight before frying. Remove the chicken from buttermilk.

Preheat the oven to 350°. Liberally salt and pepper the chicken. Heat a skillet with the oil over medium heat to about 300°. Dredge each chicken leg in the flour, and shake off excess. Put the floured chicken legs into the oil without crowding them; you'll need to do this in batches, but you are simply browning the legs, not cooking them all the way through.

Lay the browned legs in a roasting pan. Don't be afraid to pile the legs on top of each other. Bake for at least 90 minutes, up to 2 hours, covered.

Sprinkle the chicken with sea salt to finish, and enjoy the fall-apart goodness.

PREP TIME: 15 minutes COOK TIME: 7–9 minutes for fish; 30 minutes for chips YIELD: 4 servings

The Ultimate Classic Beer-Battered Fish and Chips

CHIPS
2 pounds (approximately 4) russet potatoes
2 tablespoons olive oil
1 tablespoon salt

BATTER
12 ounces your favorite beer
1½ cups all-purpose flour
½ cup cornstarch
2 tablespoons chopped fresh baby dill
1 teaspoon freshly ground black pepper
1 teaspoon salt
½ teaspoon ground cayenne pepper

FISH
1 pound firm whitefish, like halibut or cod (we use halibut for a special treat)
6 cups canola or vegetable oil, for frying
Flaky salt to finish

FOR THE CHIPS
Preheat the oven to 425°. Line a baking sheet with parchment paper. Slice the potatoes into wedges or diagonal slices resembling classic french fries, about half an inch thick. Coat with oil, and sprinkle with salt. Roast for 30 to 35 minutes, until golden brown and crisp.

FOR THE BATTER AND FISH
Whisk together all the batter ingredients; set aside. Dry the fish, and slice into 8 equal strips 1 to 1½ inches thick.

Heat the oil in a large, heavy-bottom saucepan to 350°. If you don't have a thermometer, heat the oil 7 to 9 minutes over medium to medium-high heat until it shimmers. Test the oil by dropping a bit of batter into it. If it begins to sizzle, float, and cook, you are ready to get frying. Turn the heat down if the oil hisses or begins to smoke.

Dip the fish into the batter; shake off the excess batter, and gently place the fish into the oil. Cook each piece until it's golden brown and has reached an internal temperature of 145°, or until the fish is opaque and flakes easily with a fork. It'll take 5 to 7 minutes, depending on how large the slices are.

Drain the fish on paper towels to remove excess oil, and sprinkle with salt.

CONTINUED

The Ultimate Classic Beer-Battered Fish and Chips

THE ULTIMATE TARTAR SAUCE

1 cup baby dill pickles

½ cup chopped fresh baby dill

¼ cup finely chopped red onion

1 teaspoon cracked black pepper

½ teaspoon garlic powder

Squeeze fresh lemon juice

1½ cups good mayo

SPICY KETCHUP

1 cup good ketchup

1 tablespoon malt vinegar

½ teaspoon ground cayenne
  pepper

Squeeze fresh lemon juice

FOR THE TARTAR SAUCE

Pulse first six ingredients in a food processor, and gently fold into the mayo. This keeps up to 1 week and is best made a day in advance. Store in the fridge. If you don't have a food processor, hand chop everything very finely, and fold into mayo.

FOR THE KETCHUP

Mix, and enjoy!

PREP TIME: 15 minutes COOK TIME: 20 minutes
BAKE TIME: 45 minutes YIELD: 4 servings

Puff Pastry Roast Beef Pot Pie

INGREDIENTS

2 cups beef suitable for stew, chopped into ½-inch cubes (precooked is also acceptable)

2 tablespoons butter

1 tablespoon olive oil

1 medium onion, diced

2 carrots, diced

2 medium yellow potatoes, peeled and diced

1 bay leaf

1 rib celery, diced

1 clove fresh garlic, crushed

¼ cup all-purpose flour

Salt and pepper to taste

3 cups low-sodium beef stock

1 cup milk

1 sprig fresh rosemary, whole

½ cup frozen peas

1 package puff pastry, thawed

DIRECTIONS

Preheat the oven to 350°. Brown the meat in the butter and olive oil in a large stock or soup pot over medium heat. Add the diced onion, and brown for 3 to 4 minutes. Add the carrots, potatoes, bay leaf, celery, and garlic. Cook for 3 to 4 minutes.

Add flour, salt, and pepper to taste; at this point, you are cooking the flour to make a base for the gravy. Cook for 2 minutes.

Slowly add beef stock, being careful to scrape up all the brown bits on the bottom of the pan. The mixture will thicken over a period of about 5 minutes. Add milk and rosemary. Continue cooking for 15 to 20 minutes on low heat.

When you are ready to assemble the pot pie, remove the bay leaf and rosemary stem, and add the peas. Evenly pour the meat and gravy into a baking vessel.

Lay pastry over the mixture, tightly crimping down the sides of the pastry. Bake uncovered for 30 to 45 minutes, or until the pastry is puffed and golden.

Wine-and-Tomato-Braised Short Ribs over Parmesan Cauliflower Mash

PREP TIME: 20 minutes COOK TIME: 3–4 hours YIELD: 4 servings

Wine-and-Tomato-Braised Short Ribs over Parmesan Cauliflower Mash

SHORT RIBS

3 pounds short ribs, trimmed

2 tablespoons olive oil

4 cloves fresh garlic, smashed

2 medium tomatoes, sliced

1 large yellow onion, sliced

1 cup sliced mushrooms

2 tablespoons tomato paste

Salt and pepper to taste

2 cups red wine

2 cups low-sodium beef stock or water

2 sprigs fresh rosemary

PARMESAN CAULIFLOWER MASH

2 cups chicken stock

2 pounds cauliflower (equivalent to 1 large head or 2 small heads), chopped

1 onion, sliced (any color preferred)

1½ cups heavy cream

½ cup butter

Salt and pepper to taste

1 cup grated parmesan cheese

FOR THE SHORT RIBS

Preheat the oven to 300°. Brown the short ribs in an enamel-covered Dutch oven over medium to medium-high heat in olive oil. This can be done in two batches so you don't overcrowd the pan.

Once the meat is browned, remove it and set aside. Add the garlic, tomatoes, onion, mushrooms, tomato paste, salt, and pepper to the pot.

Cook for 5 to 6 minutes, then return meat to the pan. Deglaze with wine and stock. Add rosemary, and bake for 3 to 4 hours, covered, until the meat is fall-apart tender. Check halfway through cooking, and add a little water if the liquid is low or meat is looking dry.

FOR THE PARMESAN CAULIFLOWER MASH

Bring the stock to a simmer in a large soup or stockpot over medium-high heat; add chopped cauliflower and sliced onion. Simmer until the cauliflower is falling apart and much of the stock has evaporated, about 20 minutes.

Add the heavy cream, butter, salt, and pepper. Use an immersion blender to blend until smooth and thick. Fold in the parmesan cheese. Serve hot as a base for the short ribs.

PREP TIME: 15 minutes COOK TIME: 3 hours YIELD: 4 servings

My Mom's Swiss Steak

I couldn't wait for this meal as a kid. When I was twenty-two and bought my first house, I served this to my family as the first thing I ever cooked in our new home. I made it for my husband when we were dating. I made it when my baby turned one and spooned the sauce over rice for him. I made it when my great-grandma Thora passed away. I make this simple, comforting stew when life changes and when my family needs a bit of comfort. Isn't that life? We turn to simple meals that are nourishing and filled with love. This is the kind of food you can truly feel good about. This is the kind of food you can smell as you walk up the driveway after a really long day. When we were little, my mother had only a few pots and pans. She made this in a big enamel-covered, tin turkey roaster. She made food in that until the bottom rusted out. You could cook anything in that roaster, from chickens to pot roasts and oven stews.

INGREDIENTS

2 pounds chuck steak or top round, cut into 1-inch strips
2 tablespoons olive oil
1 (27-ounce) can San Marzano tomatoes, in juice or sauce
1 cup beef stock
2 medium green bell peppers, cut into 1-inch chunks
1 medium yellow onion, sliced
3 cloves fresh garlic, smashed
1 bay leaf
2 teaspoons kosher salt
1 teaspoon freshly cracked black pepper

DIRECTIONS

Preheat the oven to 300°. Season the meat, then brown in the olive oil in an enamel-covered Dutch oven or pot suitable for braising over medium-high heat.

Once the meat is browned, season once more, add the rest of the ingredients, and bake for 3 hours.

That's it! Serve with wide egg noodles or fluffy white rice.

PREP TIME: 10 minutes COOK TIME: 90 minutes YIELD: 4 servings

Mustard Chicken Thighs and Cauliflower

VINAIGRETTE

½ cup chopped fresh parsley

¼ cup champagne vinegar

¼ cup Dijon mustard

¼ cup olive oil, suitable for
   baking

2 tablespoons honey

3 cloves fresh garlic, smashed

Salt and pepper to taste

INGREDIENTS

1 onion, sliced (any color
   preferred)

1 head cauliflower, cut into
   florets

8 chicken thighs

1 cup finely grated parmesan
   cheese

DIRECTIONS

Preheat the oven to 350°. Mix all the ingredients for the vinaigrette, including salt and pepper, in a large bowl, using a fork or whisk.

Toss in the onion and the cauliflower florets to coat, and then the chicken. Mix everything well with the vinaigrette.

Pour the entire bowl, including every last drop of vinaigrette, into a 9-by-13-inch pan (or Dutch oven with a lid). Cover the pan tightly with foil, and bake for 90 minutes.

When the dish is done baking, sprinkle the parmesan over the top, and broil uncovered for 2 to 3 minutes, until the cheese is browned and bubbly. Spoon the pan drippings over a green salad as a warm dressing.

PREP TIME: 20 minutes COOK TIME: 15–20 minutes
YIELD: 4 servings

Old-School Cracker Crumb Nuggets and Sauces

School's back in! Kids are back on schedule, and we say farewell to long summer nights. Easy, kid-friendly dinners are where it's at! What if I told you that you could make chicken nuggets that rival all other nuggets you might have tried? With whole food and ingredients and no artificial fillers? Throw in a green salad, and you've got a crowd-pleasing family dinner that doubles as awesome leftovers perfect for the lunch box.

INGREDIENTS

4 chicken breasts, cut into chunks (each breast should be trimmed and cut into 5 equal pieces, making 20 nuggets)

4 eggs

½ cup milk

2 cups all-purpose flour

1 teaspoon freshly cracked black pepper

1 teaspoon kosher salt, plus more for finishing

2 sleeves saltines or any salted water cracker, crushed

2 cups light-tasting oil, suitable for frying at 300°

Fresh flat-leaf parsley to garnish

Flaky sea salt to finish

DIRECTIONS

Gather four large bowls for the dipping stations. Put the chicken chunks into the first bowl, the eggs and milk in the second, the flour, salt, and pepper in the third, and the crushed saltines in the fourth.

Preheat the oven to 350°. Put the oil in a 12-inch frying pan or skillet, and turn the heat to just above medium. Dip 2 to 3 pieces of chicken at a time into the egg wash, then into the flour and back into the egg wash, then roll the coated chicken in the cracker crumbs. Press the crumbs firmly into the chicken, shake off the excess, and put into the hot oil.

Working quickly, you should have at least 8 to 10 nuggets in the oil at a time. Brown for 2 to 3 minutes per side, and place golden-brown nuggets on a parchment-lined baking sheet. Continue this process up to three times, refreshing the oil if needed, until each piece of chicken has been partially cooked.

Bake the chicken nuggets on the parchment-lined sheet for 15 minutes. When you remove it from the oven, sprinkle flaky sea salt and parsley all over the chicken. It's moist, crunchy, and awesome! Serve with sauces (see recipes on page 24).

CONTINUED

Old-School Cracker Crumb Nuggets and Sauces

HONEY MUSTARD

½ cup Dijon mustard

½ cup honey

2 tablespoons apple cider
vinegar

½ teaspoon garlic powder

Salt and pepper to taste

THOUSAND ISLAND

1 cup mayo

½ cup dill-pickle relish

½ cup good ketchup

2 tablespoons chopped fresh
chives

2 tablespoons white vinegar

1 tablespoon chopped fresh dill

½ teaspoon garlic powder

Salt and pepper to taste

CREAMY BBQ

½ cup your fave BBQ sauce

½ cup mayo

SOUR CREAM RANCH

1 cup good sour cream

½ cup buttermilk

1 tablespoon chopped fresh
chives

1 tablespoon chopped fresh
parsley

1 teaspoon freshly cracked
black pepper

1 teaspoon garlic powder

1 teaspoon onion powder

1 teaspoon salt

½ teaspoon dried thyme
(optional)

½ teaspoon dried rosemary
(optional)

FOR THE SAUCES

Just mix up ingredients, and enjoy! They will keep in the
refrigerator for 1 week.

PREP TIME: 5 minutes COOK TIME: 15 minutes YIELD: 4 servings

Seared Salmon with Citronette-Dressed Greens

INGREDIENTS

4–6 (6-ounce) pieces fresh
   salmon, skin on

Salt and pepper to taste

2 tablespoons olive oil

CITRONETTE

1 tablespoon good mustard

1 tablespoon honey or sugar

1 clove fresh garlic, crushed,
   not chopped

Juice and zest of 1 large or 2
   small lemons

Salt and pepper to taste

SALAD (ANY ARRAY OF FRESH GREENS WORKS)

2 heads Boston lettuce, torn

2 cups baby spinach (or pea
   vines, if you can find them)

1 bunch radishes, chopped

DIRECTIONS

Heat a large, nonstick, 12-inch skillet over medium-high heat; salt and pepper each side of the fish. Add the olive oil to the hot pan, and place the salmon in skin-side down. Cover the pan with the lid askew to allow the steam to leave and the skin to crisp; the goal is to turn the salmon only once after 4 to 5 minutes.

Flip the salmon, and watch for an additional 2 to 4 minutes, depending on desired doneness. Set finished salmon aside, and prepare the salad.

Combine all the ingredients for the citronette in a 12-ounce mason jar, and shake vigorously! Pour half the dressing over the large bowl of mixed greens, and gently toss. Dressing keeps in the fridge up to 14 days with the addition of 1 tablespoon vinegar.

To serve, simply plate up the dressed salad, and lay a piece of salmon over the top!

PREP TIME: 10 minutes COOK TIME: 25 minutes YIELD: 4 servings

Homemade Sheet-Pan Pizza

It was 1980, it was payday, my dad just got home, and my parents had paid all their bills. Rent was $180, and they had $6 left over. My mom and dad walked a mile down the road to Shakey's Pizza and ordered a bar-made special pizza: shrimp and black olives. My mother would tell us kids this story as we grew up, particularly when she made homemade pizza. Homemade dough stretched the entire surface of a baking sheet, and she always topped it with mozzarella, cheddar, plenty of browned hamburger, and loads of red sauce. Nothing tastes quite like my mom's pizza; I still feel like I'm a kid when she makes it. In all my thirty-seven years, nothing is as comforting as when Mom makes me dinner. Her stories about young love, having nothing, my dad's early cop days, and pizza with shrimp and black olives taught me about making memories around food. Memories are a slice of life, cut into squares and shared with everyone. There is such nostalgia for making pizza at home. I quite prefer it to anything else. Now that I'm a mama myself, I want to share these memories and make new ones with my sons and hubby. I bet you've had a picnic on your living-room floor with a pizza box and a bottle of wine with someone you really love. With this homemade one, all you need is dough, sauce, and toppings, and you're on your way.

INGREDIENTS

2 tablespoons oil

2 pounds your favorite pizza dough

2 cups marinara sauce

2 cups shredded mozzarella cheese

1 cup shredded cheddar cheese

1 pound ground beef, browned and seasoned with salt and pepper to taste

DIRECTIONS

Preheat the oven to 375°. Oil a half-sheet pan, and stretch the dough across the entire pan, making sure to reach the corners completely.

Spread the sauce in circles over the surface of the dough. Alternate sprinkling the cheeses and cooked ground beef in three batches. Bake for 25 to 30 minutes, until it's puffed and golden on the edges, and the cheese has bubbled.

Slice into squares, and enjoy! Feel free to add other toppings, like olives, diced green peppers, or sliced red onions.

PREP TIME: 10 minutes COOK TIME: 60 minutes YIELD: 4 sandwiches

Homestyle Meatloaf Sandwich

INGREDIENTS

2 pounds 85/15 ground beef

1 cup ketchup, divided

½ cup finely grated onion

½ cup panko bread crumbs

¼ cup brown sugar

2 eggs

2 tablespoons mustard

1 clove fresh garlic, crushed

1½ teaspoons kosher salt (I prefer this meatloaf on the salty side)

1 teaspoon garlic powder

1 teaspoon dried thyme (fresh is perfect)

1 teaspoon marjoram

1 teaspoon black pepper

½ teaspoon crushed red pepper flakes

1 dash soy sauce

SANDWICHES

6–8 ciabatta buns, sliced in half

6–8 cheese slices of preference

2–3 cups mâche lettuce or spinach

DIRECTIONS

Preheat the oven to 350°. Gently mix all the ingredients except ½ cup ketchup. Use a fork or stiff fingers—do not squish the meat together, or you might get a tough loaf. Form into a loaf in the center of a glass baking dish, and smear remaining ketchup on top.

Bake for at least 60 minutes, uncovered. I like ultra-caramelized ketchup, and this method creates a crusty tomato top that begs to be made into a sandwich! Place the loaf in the fridge to firm up for sandwich slices the next day.

FOR THE SANDWICHES

Arrange 4 slices of meatloaf on a parchment-lined baking sheet alongside 4 ciabatta buns, sliced in half and topped with cheese. Broil on high for 5 to 6 minutes. The rolls and cheese might burn, so watch them carefully; if they get too dark, pull them out.

When the meat is warmed through, place it between the cheesy ciabattas, top with mâche lettuce or spinach, and devour!

SUPPER

PREP TIME: 5 minutes COOK TIME: 5–6 hours YIELD: 4–6 servings

Apple Cider Pork Shoulder with Thyme and Sauerkraut

INGREDIENTS

- 1 3-pound boneless pork shoulder or butt
- 2 cups sauerkraut
- 1 large onion, sliced (any color preferred)
- 2 tart apples, such as Pink Lady, cored and thinly sliced
- ¾ cup apple cider vinegar
- 6 cloves fresh garlic, smashed
- 1 cup water
- 2 teaspoons kosher salt
- 2 teaspoons freshly cracked black pepper
- 2–3 sprigs fresh thyme

DIRECTIONS

Preheat the oven to 300°. Layer the ingredients in a 5-quart, enamel-coated, cast-iron Dutch oven in the order they appear. Roast for 5 to 6 hours or until the pork is fork tender.

Englevale, North Dakota. Grandma Gloria as a baby. Great-Gran Thora and Great-Grandpa Danielson.

PREP TIME: 10 minutes COOK TIME: 10 minutes YIELD: 4 servings

Angel Hair Pasta in Tomato Cream

When Noah was a baby and we didn't have very much money and I wanted to make a pasta that felt special and reminded us of running our restaurant, I'd make this simple, comforting pasta. Angel hair cooks in a matter of minutes, and the sauce comes together so quickly; there's nothing like pasta and tomatoes and cream. I am always reminded of God's provision when I make this meal. We had literally lost most of our worldly possessions, but we never lost hope or each other. I love everything that humble food represents. The cream is a definite splurge but well worth it.

INGREDIENTS

½ cup red onion, diced

¼ teaspoon crushed red pepper flakes

4 cloves fresh garlic, crushed

2 tablespoons olive oil

Salt and pepper to taste

1 (15-ounce) can diced tomatoes

1 pound dry angel hair pasta

2 cups heavy cream

½ cup grated parmesan cheese

DIRECTIONS

Sauté the onion, pepper flakes, and garlic in the olive oil in a large skillet for 3 to 4 minutes, until soft. Season with salt and pepper. Add the tomatoes, and sauté until they become jamlike and most of the juices have evaporated, about 10 minutes.

Meanwhile, cook the pasta according to package instructions in a large pot of boiled, liberally salted water. (I like to do this around the same time the tomatoes are cooked.)

Ladle the hot pasta directly from the pot into the large skillet. Toss to coat the pasta in the tomato mixture. Add the cream, and reduce the mixture. If it's too thick, add some pasta water. Taste for seasonings. Finish with fresh parmesan.

PREP TIME: 15 minutes COOK TIME: 20 minutes YIELD: 4–6 servings

Swedish-Style Meatballs in Mushroom Cream Sauce

It's a sad state of affairs when you have to gently coax your five-year-old into eating your food by comparing it to a large furniture chain's meatballs: "See, baby, these are just like said furniture store's, and I can even put a scoop of jam on your plate if you'd like!" These meatballs are life-changers for me, and now that Noah is a man at the age of eight, he requests Mom's meatballs at least once a week.

INGREDIENTS

2 pounds ground beef or turkey

2 eggs

15 saltine crackers, crushed

½ cup finely chopped fresh Italian parsley

½ cup grated parmesan cheese

1 tablespoon Dijon mustard

2 cloves fresh garlic, crushed

1½ teaspoon kosher salt

1 teaspoon onion powder

1 teaspoon freshly cracked black pepper

1 teaspoon Worcestershire sauce

1 pound cremini mushrooms, sliced

1 pound button mushrooms, sliced

1 medium onion, sliced (any color preferred)

2 tablespoons olive oil

2 cups chicken stock

2 cups heavy cream

Salt and pepper to taste

½ cup finely chopped fresh Italian parsley

DIRECTIONS

To make the meatballs, combine all the ingredients up to the mushrooms (using only half of the parsley), and gently mix, using two forks or your hands until all the ingredients are incorporated. Using both hands, roll the meat into 25 individual meatballs, roughly 2 tablespoons each, and line them up on a baking sheet. Set aside.

Sauté the mushrooms and onions in olive oil in a 12-inch nonstick skillet over medium-high heat until golden and caramelized. Remove the veggies from the pan, and set aside.

Place the meatballs in the mushroom pan, and brown on all sides (in two batches, if needed). Once the meatballs have browned, add the chicken stock, and continue to cook at a simmer. Reduce the stock by half, about 7 minutes, return the mushrooms to the pan, and add the heavy cream. Simmer over medium-low to medium heat, uncovered, for 20 minutes, until the cream has thickened and the meat is completely cooked.

Season with salt and pepper. Just before serving, add the remaining Italian parsley. Makes 25 large meatballs.

PREP TIME: 5 minutes COOK TIME: 20 minutes YIELD: 4 servings

Turkey Gravy

When I was a kid, cream of mushroom soup in a can was king. Mushroom gravy is sort of a thing in this book—at least six or seven suppers start out with it! This dinner comes together in no time at all, and there is no need to stock the pantry with canned soup. My homemade gravy is the best part.

This recipe is so easily adapted, you can use any ground meat you love. When I was young, my family always ate it with hamburger, but now we love it with ground turkey.

INGREDIENTS

1 pound ground turkey

2 tablespoons olive oil

2 tablespoons butter

1 medium onion, diced (any
color preferred)

2 cups finely diced button
mushrooms

2 cups chopped spinach

¼ cup all-purpose flour

2 cloves fresh garlic, crushed

4 cups milk

2 cups chicken stock

1 cup grated parmesan cheese

Salt and pepper to taste

DIRECTIONS

Brown the turkey in the olive oil and butter in a large soup pot. Remove from the pan, and sauté the onions, mushrooms, and spinach until caramelized, about 7 minutes.

Return the turkey to the pot, adding the flour and garlic. Cook the mixture for 2 to 3 minutes, until the flour is cooked. Slowly add the milk and stock. Bring the gravy to a simmer, and cook for 20 minutes over medium heat, stirring constantly.

Remove from heat, and add the parmesan. Serve over rice.

PREP TIME: 30 minutes COOK TIME: 40 minutes YIELD: 4 servings

Shepherd's Pie

My sister, Jenny, is the shepherd's pie queen. She lived in Missouri for seven years while her husband was in the air force and developed a really special love for Midwestern and Southern cooking. She makes this tasty pie, and we all love it.

INGREDIENTS

4–5 medium Yukon Gold potatoes, diced

1 cup heavy cream

1 cup grated parmesan cheese

1 pound ground beef

1 medium onion, diced

2 tablespoons butter

2 medium carrots, diced

2 cloves fresh garlic, crushed

2 cups beef stock

1 cup frozen corn

1 cup frozen peas

2 tablespoons cornstarch

2 tablespoons hot water

DIRECTIONS

Preheat the oven to 350°. Cover the potatoes with water in a medium pot, and bring to a boil. Boil for about 30 minutes until they are fork tender.

Drain, and roughly mash with the cream and parmesan; set aside.

Brown the hamburger and onion in the butter; add the carrots, garlic, and stock, and cook for 5 to 7 minutes, until the carrots are tender. Add frozen veggies.

Make a slurry with the cornstarch and hot water, and pour the slurry into the meat mixture; it will become glossy and thicken slightly.

Pour contents into a 9-by-13-inch pan, and cover with mashed potatoes. Make sure to have plenty of peaks and valleys in the potatoes to crisp up in the oven. Bake for 20 minutes, uncovered.

SUPPER 35

Stovetop Mac 'n' Cheese

PREP TIME: 10 minutes COOK TIME: 10 minutes YIELD: 4 servings

Stovetop Mac 'n' Cheese

This dish is a trick from my restaurant days. We'd make elaborate pastas on the line that used only heavy cream to thicken the base. What, no roux? No flour? Could this actually be? Oh yes, yes it can. I prefer these creamy, cheesy noodles to ANY you'd find with a flour-thickened base. My Noah asks for them all the time, and they don't need a second bake. This dish is on the table in under 15 minutes.

INGREDIENTS

1 pound uncooked short pasta

3 cups heavy cream

1 tablespoon butter

1 teaspoon Dijon mustard

½ teaspoon ground cayenne pepper

1 cup shredded sharp cheddar cheese

1 cup shredded parmesan cheese

1 cup shredded gruyère cheese

Salt and pepper to taste

BUTTERY BREAD CRUMB TOPPING

2 slices country bread

2 tablespoons melted butter

¼ cup chopped parsley

¼ teaspoon garlic powder

Salt and pepper to taste

FOR THE BREAD CRUMBS

Toast the bread, and butter each side. Chop the bread and parsley together and put in a bowl. Sprinkle the garlic powder on the bread, and add any remaining butter and a pinch of salt and pepper. Mix.

FOR THE MAC 'N' CHEESE

Bring 6 quarts of salted water to a boil. Cook the pasta according to the directions on the package. Drain the pasta, and return to the stove on low heat. Add the cream, butter, mustard, and cayenne to the pot, and mix thoroughly.

Remove the pot from the heat, and add cheeses; mix until they're melted. Taste for salt and pepper. Sprinkle Buttery Bread Crumbs on top, and enjoy.

SUPPER 37

PREP TIME: 15 minutes COOK TIME: 2–3 hours YIELD: 4 servings

Smothered Chicken and Mushroom Gravy

Mushroom gravy was the backbone of our cooking when I was growing up. When I set out to write this book, I took every tradition and made it wholesome. I took scratch recipes and stepped back in time, trading canned cream soups for homemade gravies. My mom poured mushroom gravy over her scalloped potatoes. My dad's favorite chicken on the bone is smothered in this flavorful gravy, and it's the star in hamburger gravy over rice. It's so simple and flavorful, I'm sure I could find *a million uses for this base*. The summer of my junior year in high school, my great-gran Thora came to stay with us. We had a sweet thousand-square-foot home, so my sister and I shared a room. I slept on the couch for three weeks, my sister slept on the floor of my parents' room, and Great-Gran took over our room. My mother talked about the magical food Great-Gran made when she was young. When she visited, she was well into her eighties, but she made my dad's favorite smothered chicken and mashers and an apple pie for dessert. There is nothing more beautiful than watching a pair of well-worn hands make pie crust. Her fingers bent in a way that you get only by working hard and living for many decades. She gently cut cold butter into the flour and made two separate disks. We had a tiny kitchen, and she mixed the dough in a large metal bowl and rolled it out on our dining-room table. What I wouldn't give to be back in that kitchen; it was the only time in my life I got to watch her cook. She passed away just a few years later. She left such a legacy that came from her hands and lives on today. More than cooking, there is a legacy of hope and love. I love to hear my mother talk about her: a true matriarch in every sense of the word.

Great Falls, Montana. Great-Gran Thora, Grandma Gloria, Great-Aunt Pat, and Great-Auntie Charlotte.

CONTINUED

Smothered Chicken and Mushroom Gravy

INGREDIENTS

1 whole chicken, cut into
8 pieces, excess skin or
cartilage removed

2 tablespoons olive oil

6 cups whole milk

1 pound mushrooms, diced

1 large onion, diced (any color
preferred)

½ cup butter

2 cloves fresh garlic, crushed

¼ cup all-purpose flour

1 cup chopped flat-leaf parsley
or spinach

Salt and pepper to taste

DIRECTIONS

Preheat the oven to 300°. Brown the chicken in the olive oil in a
large skillet, then generously salt and pepper, remove from pan,
and set aside.

Dump the mushrooms and onion into the pan; once the
vegetables have browned, melt the butter in the pan, add garlic,
and cook until frothy and bubbly (2 to 3 minutes). Stir in the
flour quickly. Cook at least 3 minutes to remove raw-flour taste.

Warm the milk in a separate saucepan. Slowly stir the hot milk
into the butter-and-flour mixture and thicken, seasoning as
needed.

Put the chicken in a baking vessel with a lid (I like a roasting
pan or Dutch oven), and pour the gravy over it. Bake for 2 to 3
hours. Garnish with parsley or spinach.

Serve with mashed potatoes or buttered noodles.

PREP TIME: 10 minutes COOK TIME: 15 minutes YIELD: 4 servings

Garlic Butter Shrimp

INGREDIENTS

2 pounds large 16–20 count shrimp

½ cup butter, cut into pieces

1 tablespoon olive oil

10 cloves fresh garlic, smashed

1 pinch crushed red pepper flakes or a fresh diced Fresno chili

Pepper to taste

½ cup chopped flat-leaf parsley

Salt to taste

DIRECTIONS

Preheat a 12-inch skillet over medium-high heat. Peel and devein the shrimp. Melt butter and oil in the hot skillet, add garlic, pepper flakes, and pepper, then sauté for 1 to 2 minutes before adding the shrimp.

Add the shrimp and cook for 3 to 4 minutes, turning each shrimp over at least once halfway through cooking. The shrimp are done when each piece is pink and the shape of a C.

Season with salt and add the parsley. Sauté for another 30 seconds and serve with any greens you like.

PREP TIME: 10 min YIELD: 4 servings

Fresh Crab Feast

INGREDIENTS

2 or 3 large Dungeness crabs, cooked

1 stick butter, melted

1 (15-ounce) bottle prepared cocktail sauce (you can make your own, but I don't mind the bottled stuff)

1 lemon, wedged

DIRECTIONS

Spread an old newspaper all over a table. Set small bowls of the melted butter and the cocktail sauce at each place setting. Lay out scissors and nutcrackers.

To clean the crab, simply lift off the top shell, placing fingers under the back lip of the shell. Clean out inner cavity, and break the crab into halves. Put him in the go-ahead-and-eat pile!

Repeat this process as many times as needed for every crab. Garnish with lemon wedges. Tell guests to grab a crab, and eat!

PREP TIME: 5 minutes COOK TIME: 15–20 minutes YIELD: 4 servings

Toasted Pimento Cheese Sandwiches

INGREDIENTS

- 2 cups shredded sharp cheddar cheese
- 1 cup shredded parmesan cheese
- 8 ounces cream cheese, softened
- 1½ cups mayonnaise
- 1 cup fire-roasted red peppers, well drained and diced
- Salt and pepper to taste
- ½ cup butter, softened
- 8 slices crusty sourdough bread or other artisan loaf, like ciabatta or pugliese

DIRECTIONS

Mix the cheeses, mayo, peppers, and seasoning in the bowl of a stand mixer or with a hand mixer on the lowest setting. Generously butter one side of each slice of bread. Heat a skillet over medium heat (a lower temp for longer will yield a crunchy, nicely melted sammie).

Spread a heaping few tablespoons of the cheese mix on the non-buttered side of the bread, top with another slice of bread (butter facing out), and place the sandwich in the hot pan.

Cook for 3 to 4 minutes on each side. If the bread begins to brown too quickly, lower the heat.

Nelscott, Oregon. Great-Gran Thora and Great-Grandpa Danielson.

PREP TIME: 15 minutes COOK TIME: 60 minutes YIELD: 4 servings

Sheet-Pan Chicken and Carrots

INGREDIENTS

2 tablespoons olive oil

10 carrots, washed, peeled, and sliced on the bias

2 medium onions, sliced (any color preferred)

Salt and pepper to taste

5 sprigs fresh thyme, whole

1 whole chicken, backbone removed (see note)

DIRECTIONS

Preheat the oven to 375°. Combine all the ingredients except the chicken in a large mixing bowl; mix well to coat the vegetables.

Spread veggies and herbs onto a large baking sheet with a rim. Lay chicken on top of the carrots and onions, breast-side up. Run any oil remaining in the bowl on the chicken. Sprinkle liberally with salt and pepper. Bake for 60 minutes.

Halfway through, use a spatula to turn the vegetables once. Don't worry about veggies under the chicken. The chicken is done when the juices run clear after a knife is inserted between the thigh and breast.

Note: Most grocery-store butchers will cut the backbone out of the chicken for you. If not, use kitchen shears to cut along either side of the backbone to remove it.

PREP TIME: 10 minutes COOK TIME: 20 minutes YIELD: 4–6 servings

Sloppy Joes

INGREDIENTS

1½ pounds ground beef

1 medium onion, diced (any color preferred)

4 cloves fresh garlic, smashed

1 teaspoon ground turmeric

1 teaspoon onion powder

2 cups low-sodium beef stock or broth

1 green bell pepper, diced

1 (6-ounce) can tomato paste

2 generous tablespoons dark brown sugar

2 teaspoons tamari or soy sauce

1 generous teaspoon brown or Dijon mustard

1 good dash hot sauce, preferably vinegar based

6 sandwich buns (I prefer brioche)

Butter for the bread

DIRECTIONS

Brown the ground beef and onion in a heavy-bottomed skillet over medium heat. Add the smashed garlic and seasonings, and cook for 2 to 3 minutes. Add the rest of the ingredients (except the bread and butter), and bring to a simmer. The meat sauce will begin to thicken and develop a richer color; I cook it for about 20 minutes.

Spread a bit of butter on each bun, and toast under the broiler for 2 minutes to lightly brown. Spoon the meat sauce over the buns, and serve with a crunchy green salad.

PREP TIME: 15 minutes COOK TIME: 65–75 minutes YIELD: 4 servings

Mustard-Roasted Chicken and Potatoes

INGREDIENTS

6 Yukon Gold potatoes,
  unpeeled

½ cup chicken stock

½ cup light olive oil

½ cup whole-grain mustard

3 cloves fresh garlic, smashed
  and chopped

1 tablespoon fresh lemon juice

1 tablespoon chopped fresh
  rosemary

1 teaspoon freshly cracked
  black pepper

½ teaspoon kosher salt

6–8 boneless, skinless chicken
  thighs (about 1½ pounds)

DIRECTIONS

Preheat the oven to 375°. Put the potatoes in a medium soup pot, and cover with water. Bring to a boil for 15 minutes.

Meanwhile, whisk together all the remaining ingredients (except the chicken, of course) to make the dressing.

To assemble, quarter the potatoes, and lay them in the bottom of a glass baking dish no larger than 9-by-13 inches.

Arrange the chicken thighs on the potatoes. Pour dressing over the chicken and potatoes, taking care to get dressing on every potato and chicken thigh. Cover tightly with foil, and bake for 30 minutes.

Remove the foil and finish cooking, uncovered, for 30 to 45 minutes, until the chicken is tender and falls apart and the potatoes are soft and caramelized.

PREP TIME: 15 minutes COOK TIME: 35 minutes YIELD: 4 servings

Company Chicken

Growing up, we used those beefy onion-soup packets for roasts, soups, and stews. I don't buy so many seasoning packets these days, because I have discovered how to make food taste good using real stuff, like onions and beef stock! This chicken is such a treat, and my family gobbles it up.

My aunt Christy makes this, and I believe the recipe first came from my uncle Lee's mother, Vicki. So here's to you, Vicki; we can't get enough of your chicken. Something just a little sweet to remember her by.

INGREDIENTS

8 boneless, skinless chicken thighs

2 tablespoons olive oil

4 medium onions, sliced (any color preferred)

½ cup tamari or soy sauce (but tamari really sets this dish off)

½ cup apricot jam

2 tablespoons water or freshly squeezed orange juice

2 cloves fresh garlic, crushed

1 pinch crushed red pepper flakes

DIRECTIONS

Preheat the oven to 350°. In an oven-proof skillet (I prefer a 12-inch, cast-iron one), sear the chicken on both sides in olive oil. (I skip salt in this recipe because the tamari has enough to season the entire dish.)

Remove the chicken from the pan, and add the sliced onion. Caramelize the onions in pan drippings over medium heat; nestle the chicken on top of the onions.

In a bowl, mix the tamari, jam, juice or water, garlic, and pepper flakes, and pour the sauce over the chicken and onions. Bake uncovered for 35 minutes. The longer you cook it, the stickier and more delicious your sauce will be. (You can never overcook a chicken thigh, in my opinion; cover the skillet with foil if it looks as if it's browning too quickly in the oven.)

Serve over rice or steamed broccoli.

SUPPER 47

Baked Chicken Parmesan

PREP TIME: 20 minutes COOK TIME: 25 minutes YIELD: 4 servings

Baked Chicken Parmesan

FRESH MARINARA

2 pounds on-the-vine tomatoes,
   chopped
1 large onion, chopped (any
   color preferred)
1 cup chicken stock
½ cup chopped fresh basil
2 cloves fresh garlic, chopped
Salt and pepper to taste

INGREDIENTS

3 chicken breasts, butterflied
   and sliced in half
about ½ cup light olive oil
   (enough for a shallow fry)
Salt and pepper to taste
1 egg, beaten
1 cup all-purpose flour
1½ cups shredded mozzarella
   cheese
1 cup grated parmesan

DIRECTIONS

Preheat the oven to 350°. Combine all the ingredients for the
Fresh Marinara in a medium saucepan, and bring to a simmer
over medium heat. Simmer for at least 20 minutes.

For the chicken, heat the skillet and oil over medium heat to
300°. Season the 6 pieces of chicken liberally with salt and
pepper. Dip the chicken in the beaten egg, and press gently into
the flour.

Lay the chicken gently into the oil; brown it, but don't cook
it fully. Once the chicken is browned on both sides, lay it in a
9-by-13-inch baking dish.

Spoon the marinara over each piece of chicken (but don't drown
them); reserve some for serving. Cover with the mozzarella and
parmesan and bake uncovered for 25 minutes, until the cheese
is melty and the chicken is fully cooked. Serve with fresh pasta,
and spoon more sauce over top.

PREP TIME: 20 minutes COOK TIME: 90 minutes YIELD: 4 servings

Olive Chicken

Entrepreneur.

At the time, I didn't know what it was or even how to spell it, but I was somehow living it as a kid. Some things seem to start things.

I always knew I was different. I used to sell candy out of my backpack in junior high. I made earrings out of paper clips and rode my bike to the fabric store to buy beads to peddle. I never felt like I couldn't do anything, and I always felt as old as I am now. I had this vision that I could do things in my life. I knew the world was huge, and I couldn't wait to see and feel every part of it. I had no patience for taking my time; I felt that life was limitless.

I am happy to report that even through every one of my failed endeavors and closed-down businesses, I'd find my calling in life. I still feel like life is limitless. No matter who you are or where you came from, you can be anything you want to be here in the USA. We are so profoundly blessed by freedom. I have failed so much; I will continue to fail and mess up and do it all wrong, but every so often, we get it right. I live for the process. There is no next best thing. It's truly all about the process, the experience in attempting another goal. It brings me joy to be with people and live every day to its fullest.

This chicken dish was one of the first meals I learned to make that really wowed people. I can remember the week I made it at my mother's house; I was in my early twenties, maybe twenty-one, and I hadn't yet moved into my own home. I had just seen on TV that you could sear a chicken breast and finish the cooking in the oven. My mind was blown. I had to try it! I know I was of drinking age, because I went to the grocery store and bought a bottle of white wine. I was going to try something crazy.

This was truly a departure from all the food we ate growing up. I seared about eight chicken breasts and put them in the bottom of a large roaster. I began to dig through the pantry and fridge. What could go in here? Olives! Onions! Tomatoes! Wine! I sautéed the onions in the pan drippings, and things started to really get brown. Here goes nothing: I deglazed the pan! Thank you, Food Network. It sputtered and bubbled, and I was so nervous. It started to calm down, and I began adding everything that made sense. In went capers and a can of stewed tomatoes, chopped zucchini, and even carrots. The stars were the briny olives. I mounted the sauce with butter (yes, channel nine taught me this). It thickened slightly, and I reduced it for about fifteen minutes. I poured the sauce over the top of the chicken, covered it, and put the roaster in the oven. I had no idea what was going to happen, but it all made sense. I thought, *It has to work.*

SUPPER   51

CONTINUED

Olive Chicken

It baked for a long time, maybe an hour or an hour and a half. The house smelled like heaven! I sprinkled parmesan cheese over the top and served it with pasta. My family was amazed! This quickly became one of our family's favorite foods; I cooked it for anyone and everyone. For years, it was the only thing I really cooked well. I had no idea at the time that I would have a career in food ten years later, but this was the dish that started it all for me. I couldn't get enough of cooking; I wanted to try to taste everything I'd never heard of before. I had never seen a fig or butternut squash growing up. I thought there were only two kinds of lettuce: iceberg and romaine!

This dish represents all the failures and all the successes in my life. It truly is something so simple and special, and when I taste it, I am reminded of what God has done in my life. You can feel that way about the Lord by eating chicken? Yes, my sweet friends, you truly can.

Food has a way of leading us back to who we are meant to be. This dish will forever be my favorite. It started so many other dishes, and it taught me to just go for it. The outcome might just be brilliant. Many, many failed dishes followed this one, but so many things I tried worked. This started a quest to learn the why behind cooking. For years, I copied my mother and didn't know why I was doing something; it was just the way she did it. I started to understand that there were methods to foolproof cooking.

Thank you, olives and chicken and Jesus. Never stop trying, always push forward, and feel free to fail. God didn't make you to sit on the sidelines; He made you to do only that one thing that you can. Do you know no one can do it like you? You are just that special and just that needed. Make this dish. It might spark something fiery inside you.

CONTINUED

Olive Chicken

INGREDIENTS

4 boneless, skinless chicken
breasts, butterflied

4 boneless, skinless chicken
thighs

2 tablespoons olive oil

1 medium onion, sliced (any
color preferred)

2 cups white wine

1 (15-ounce) can diced
tomatoes

1 cup black olives (see note)

1 cup green olives

½ cup capers, drained and
rinsed

4 cloves fresh garlic, crushed

1 pinch crushed red pepper
flakes

Salt and pepper to taste

¼ cup cold butter, cut into
cubes

DIRECTIONS

Preheat the oven to 350°. Brown each side of all the chicken pieces in olive oil. You aren't looking to cook the chicken, just get it some caramelized color.

Lay the browned chicken in an enamel-covered Dutch oven or a lidded roasting pan, and add the sliced onion to the skillet you browned the chicken in. Cook for 2 to 3 minutes, then use the wine to deglaze the pan. Scrape any brown bits off the bottom of the pan; it should be nice and hot, around medium-high heat. Add the rest of the ingredients except the butter. Reduce sauce for 10 minutes.

Add butter, and stir constantly to thicken slightly. Pour the sauce and veggies over the chicken, and cover with a lid. Bake for 90 minutes.

The chicken will be fall-apart tender and oh so perfect. Serve with fresh pasta.

Note: Most grocery stores have olive bars these days, with roasted garlic, multiple kinds of olives, and pickled or briny veggies and peppers. Load up a container for this dish. Eight to ten dollars a pound may seem steep, but it'll save you money in the long run, since you don't have to buy multiple jars of things.

Soups and Stews

Odds and Ends Can Make Brilliance

We were poor when I was little. Oh my goodness, am I grateful for that. I got to learn how to shop and how to take care of things from a young age. I got to appreciate how much a dollar was worth, and I learned how to use up all our food. There was very little food waste in our home as a kid. I also don't remember anyone being terribly picky; we all just seemed to eat what my mom made. When supplies would get slim, we made soup. Somehow, we could always make a big pot of soup. My mom never used broth or stock, always water. We relied on the bit of goodness in the pan to create a rich and wonderful broth.

One day, my parents were out, and I really wanted to impress my folks. It was a particularly hard time in our lives financially, and we kids knew we didn't have lots of money, but we absolutely never suffered. We made the most of it. We had virtually nothing in the fridge on this particular day, but there always seemed to be a little onion and celery, a can of stewed tomatoes, and lentils. Always a bit of rice in the cupboard. The original version had no meat, but these days, I brown a pound of ground turkey, chicken, or beef. We had a taco-seasoning packet, and I used that and the lentils to make a hearty and wonderful soup. I remember enlisting my sister to break the taco shells in half, and in half again, to resemble chips. We had a feast, and my mom was very impressed. This soup means victory to me.

There is always just a little more you can do, even when situations are tough and all you've got left are odds and ends. Sometimes, those little bits of goodness add up to one big, fulfilling pot.

PREP TIME: 15 minutes COOK TIME: 2½ hours YIELD: 4 servings

Bacon and White Bean Soup

What's the difference between soup and stew? Essentially, soup is, well, soupy. It's got a lot more liquid or broth for your ingredients to swim around in. A stew is more like a braise, so it doesn't need as much liquid, and it's cooked longer. Soup comes together really quickly. This one is a weeknight favorite: serve it up with crusty bread, and you're done. The key to a flavorful soup is a wonderful broth base that you can create in no time with good caramelization at the bottom of your pan.

INGREDIENTS

1 pound lightly smoked bacon

2 sprigs fresh rosemary, whole

2 sprigs fresh thyme, whole

1 medium onion, diced (any color preferred)

3 cloves fresh garlic, crushed

3 ribs celery, diced

2 carrots, diced

1 Delicata squash, sliced into half-moons, seeds removed

1 bunch kale, ribs removed, chopped

1 zucchini, diced

6 cups chicken broth

Ham bone (optional)

2 (15-ounce) cans navy beans, rinsed and drained

Fresh lemon juice and grated parmesan cheese for garnish

DIRECTIONS

Put sliced bacon and woodsy herbs in a cold pan, along with onion. Render most of the fat from the bacon so it retains some texture once you add the broth; otherwise, you'll get fatty, limp bacon and no real depth of flavor. Those brown bits will develop on the bottom of the pan as you render the bacon.

Drain half the fat, and add the garlic and the rest of the veggies. Add the broth (and ham bone, if you managed to put it in your freezer at the last holiday gathering; if you don't have a ham bone squirreled away, skip it). Bring to a simmer, then reduce heat to low, and cook for 20 minutes. Gently nudge those brown bits of flavor off the bottom of the pan with a wooden spoon. This can cook for up to 2 hours.

Add the beans during the last 5 minutes of cooking along with a squeeze of fresh lemon juice and a sprinkling of fresh parmesan over the top of the soup.

SOUPS AND STEWS 57

PREP TIME: 15 minutes COOK TIME: 60 minutes YIELD: 4 servings

Hamburger Soup

If I could pick one iconic, humble meal that *made* me, it'd be this simple, nourishing hamburger soup. We had it at least once a week growing up, and I never grew tired of it. It was always comprised of whatever veggies we had hanging out in the crisper; sometimes it'd have cabbage or yellow squash, and sometimes it'd be meat and corn and potatoes. Any way you make this, it's wonderful. I can close my eyes and see my mom filling the pot full of water; as it boiled, the heavenly soup was born. I don't even use chicken stock in this soup; I let the meat and veggies make a lovely broth. My mom used to drain and rinse all the hamburger after it'd been browned. I don't do that. I keep all the fat in for more flavor.

INGREDIENTS

1 pound 85/15 ground beef

1 large onion, chopped (any color preferred)

5 yellow potatoes, diced

3 ribs celery, chopped

2 cups frozen corn

2 cups frozen green beans

1 zucchini, chopped

1 (15-ounce) can stewed tomatoes

2 teaspoons garlic powder

2 teaspoons onion powder

Salt and pepper to taste

8–10 cups water, depending on the size of your pot

DIRECTIONS

Brown the hamburger in a large soup pot; do not drain the fat.

Add all the chopped veggies and seasonings. Cover with water and bring to a boil, then reduce to a low simmer for 45 to 60 minutes. The longer you cook it, the more delicious it becomes.

58 SOUPS AND STEWS

PREP TIME: 15 minutes COOK TIME: 90 minutes YIELD: 4 servings

Real Baked Potato Soup

This is such a great soup because we basically are making a super-cheesy béchamel sauce and topping it with all the potato fixings. It's a big ole bowl of cheesy potato goodness!

INGREDIENTS

4 russet potatoes

12 slices thick-cut bacon

½ cup butter

1 pinch crushed red pepper flakes

Salt and pepper to taste

¼ cup all-purpose flour

6 cups whole milk

2 cups chicken stock

3 cups grated sharp cheddar cheese (reserve 1 cup)

1 cup grated parmesan cheese

2 cups sliced green onions

1 cup sour cream

DIRECTIONS

Preheat the oven to 375°. Use a fork to make two sets of vent holes in each potato, and tightly wrap them in foil. Bake for 60 minutes.

When the potatoes have about 20 minutes left, put bacon on a baking sheet, and bake for the remaining time alongside the potatoes.

FOR THE CREAMY SOUP

Melt the butter; add the red pepper flakes, salt, pepper, and flour. Cook for 3 minutes. Add the milk and stock, and stir constantly. Bring to a simmer for 10 minutes. Remove from heat, and add the cheeses; the sauce should be thick, flavorful, and creamy.

By this time, the potatoes and bacon should be cooked. Dice them, along with the green onions. Add the potatoes to the soup and stir. (I like to set up an assembly line with all the toppings: the reserved cheddar cheese, bacon, green onions, and sour cream.) This is a really fun and unexpected way to enjoy Real Baked Potato Soup.

SOUPS AND STEWS

PREP TIME: 15 minutes COOK TIME: 1 hour 15 minutes
YIELD: 4 servings

Bouillabaisse or Fish Stew

INGREDIENTS

2 tablespoons oil

2 tablespoons butter

1 medium onion, chopped (any color preferred)

3 heads garlic, peeled and smashed

2 teaspoons kosher salt

1 teaspoon dried paprika

1 teaspoon freshly ground black pepper

1 (28-ounce) can crushed tomatoes (unsalted)

3 cups your favorite white wine

2 cups chicken stock

1 pound steamer clams

1 pound petrale sole or any whitefish, two-inch cubes

1 pound shrimp

Lemon and parsley for garnish

Crusty bread, cut into hunks, for serving

DIRECTIONS

Sweat the onions and garlic in the oil and butter in a large pot over medium heat. Add the spices, and continue cooking for 3 to 4 minutes.

Add the tomatoes, wine, and stock, and simmer covered for 1 hour.

Add the steamer clams; after 3 more minutes, add whitefish chunks and shrimp. Cook covered, and stir very gently for another 3 to 4 minutes, until clams have opened and the shrimp and fish are opaque.

Serve in big soup bowls with lemon wedges, fresh parsley, and hunks of crusty bread for dipping.

SOUPS AND STEWS 61

Classic Oven–Braised Beef and Tomato Stew over Cream Cheese Polenta

62

PREP TIME: 20 minutes COOK TIME: 3 hours YIELD: 4–6 servings

Classic Oven-Braised Beef and Tomato Stew over Cream Cheese Polenta

INGREDIENTS

- 2 pounds chuck roast, trimmed and cut into 2-inch cubes
- 2–3 tablespoons olive oil suitable for frying
- 5 strips thick center-cut bacon, diced
- 1 large onion, roughly chopped
- 3 cups chopped on-the-vine tomatoes
- 2 cups cremini mushrooms, cleaned
- 2 teaspoons kosher salt
- 1 teaspoon freshly cracked black pepper
- 1 pinch crushed red pepper flakes
- ¼ cup tomato paste
- 2 cups red wine
- 1 cup water or low-/no-sodium beef stock
- 2–3 sprigs fresh rosemary, whole

DIRECTIONS

Preheat the oven to 300°. Brown the meat in batches over medium to medium-high heat in the olive oil until each side is golden and caramelized but not cooked in the center; set aside. Add the bacon and onion to the pan, and brown for 5 to 7 minutes over medium heat.

Add the rest of the veggies and seasonings and cook for about 5 minutes. Add the tomato paste to coat everything. Return the meat and its juices back to the oven-safe pot, and mix everything together; deglaze the pan with the wine and stock. Add the rosemary, and bake with the lid on 3–5 hours.

This stew is finished at 3 hours but tastes better the longer it spends in the oven. Check on the liquid in the pot halfway through cooking; add water in 1-cup increments if needed. Serve with Cream Cheese Polenta (see recipe on page 107).

PREP TIME: 15 minutes COOK TIME: 45 minutes YIELD: 4 servings

Potato, Parsnip, and Celeriac Root Vegetable Soup

INGREDIENTS

6 yellow potatoes, chopped

4 quarts low-sodium chicken stock

2 parsnips, chopped

2 cups peeled and cubed celeriac root

2 cups water

1 large yellow onion, chopped

4 cloves fresh garlic

2 teaspoons kosher salt

1 teaspoon freshly cracked black pepper

½ cup heavy cream

Pan-roasted mushrooms for garnish (optional)

Bread crumbs for garnish (optional)

½ cup toasted pepitas (optional)

DIRECTIONS

Combine all the ingredients except the heavy cream and garnishes in a large stockpot. Simmer for about 45 minutes on medium-high heat until all veggies are tender and perhaps even falling apart. Taste for seasoning; adjust.

Remove the soup from the heat. Use an immersion blender to gently pulse the soup until it's your desired consistency (I prefer a thicker soup). Feel free to use a blender if that's what you have on hand, but be very careful.

Just before serving, swirl the cream into the soup, but do not mix it fully; the remnants of cream swirls look lovely. Garnish with more pepper, pan-roasted mushrooms, bread crumbs, or pepitas.

PREP TIME: 15 minutes COOK TIME: 30–45 minutes YIELD: 4 servings

Curried Carrot Soup

> This soup reminds me to step out. Sometimes stepping out feels wrong—like you need to hurry back home to the normal way of doing things. I made this recipe for one of my workshops, and I have to say I had never made it before that, but I just knew in my heart all the flavors would mingle perfectly. God made each of us to do very special things; He made us to be different from everyone else. I know that life gets hard, and we get sick, and we lose jobs, and we miss opportunities, but I have to tell you that you were made to do hard things. I had never hosted an event in New York. I had never even set foot in Brooklyn or stood in Times Square before fall of 2016. I can remember packing for that trip: it felt surreal. People were flying from all over the country to spend the weekend with our team and learn what we had to offer in the way of photography and food styling. I packed my favorite curry paste in my suitcase in Bubble Wrap. The entire trip was an exercise in faith: I had meetings at CBS, Food52, and the Food Network. I remember knowing that I just needed to step out. That trip changed my career.
>
> When you are feeling lost or afraid, take the path less traveled. When I was in seventh grade, I had a teacher who read the famous Robert Frost poem to our class; I vividly remember hearing it for the first time. I promised my twelve-year-old self that would always be me: I would always choose the path less traveled; I would always choose the adventure, pack up that curry paste, and make the soup. It might just be the most nourishing thing you've ever done. It might just change your life.

Oaks, North Dakota. Great-great-great Grandma and Grandpa Pederson. Grandma Gloria, second from right.

SOUPS AND STEWS 67

CONTINUED

Curried Carrot Soup

INGREDIENTS

2 medium yellow onions, sliced

3 tablespoons red Indian-style
curry paste

2 tablespoons olive oil

4 cloves fresh garlic, smashed

1 bay leaf

2 pounds carrots, skin on,
washed and chopped

2 parsnips, skin on, washed and
chopped

1 (27-ounce) can San Marzano
tomatoes

2–3 cups chicken stock

Salt and pepper to taste

1 (15-ounce) can coconut
cream, full-fat coconut milk,
or heavy cream

½ teaspoon crushed red pepper
flakes

Toasted pepitas, cream, and
fresh herbs to garnish

DIRECTIONS

Sauté the onions in the curry paste and olive oil in a large soup
pot or Dutch oven over medium heat until translucent, 5 to 7
minutes; add garlic and bay leaf.

Add carrots, parsnips, tomatoes, chicken stock, and salt and
pepper. Bring to a simmer with the lid on for 30 minutes, until
the veggies are tender.

Remove the bay leaf. Use an immersion blender to blend the
soup until smooth. Add coconut milk, and check for salt; add
red pepper flakes and additional seasonings if needed. If the
soup is too thick, add another cup of chicken stock; if it's too
thin, reduce it uncovered for an additional 15 minutes.

Garnish with toasted pepitas, cream, and fresh herbs.

PREP TIME: 10 minutes COOK TIME: 4–6 hours YIELD: 6–8 cups

Perfect Chicken Stock

INGREDIENTS

Cooked or roasted bones of 2 chickens
2 quarts water
3 onions, skin and all
3 carrots, stems and all
1 head garlic, sliced in half
1 bunch parsley
2 bay leaves
2 teaspoons kosher salt
1 teaspoon cracked black pepper

DIRECTIONS

Bring all the ingredients to a boil in a large stockpot, then reduce the heat to low, and simmer covered for 4 to 6 hours.

Strain and discard the contents, and reserve the stock for all your cooking projects. This stock freezes excellently and is best used within three months of the freeze date.

Russelville, Oregon. Grandma Gloria, Great-Auntie Charlotte, and Great-Aunt Pat.

SOUPS AND STEWS 69

PREP TIME: 15 minutes **COOK TIME:** 30 minutes **YIELD:** 4–6 servings

Classic New England Clam Chowder Bread Bowls

INGREDIENTS

6 slices thick-cut bacon, diced

4 medium Yukon Gold potatoes, diced

2 ribs celery, diced

2 carrots, diced

1 medium yellow onion, diced

2 tablespoons butter

2 teaspoons kosher salt

1 teaspoon cracked black pepper

1 teaspoon dried thyme

1 bay leaf

½ teaspoon white pepper

¼ cup all-purpose flour

3 (6.5-ounce) cans razor clams in clam juice, or 1 pound fresh razor clams

6 cups no-salt-added chicken stock (low-sodium is fine)

Milk, for consistency, as needed

2 cups half-and-half or heavy cream

½ cup minced fresh parsley

Bread bowls for serving (see note)

DIRECTIONS

Brown the bacon in a large heavy-bottomed soup pot or Dutch oven over medium heat. The slower you cook the bacon, the more crisp your results.

Once the bacon is browned (5 to 7 minutes), add the vegetables, butter, and seasonings. Sauté for 4 to 5 minutes, then add the flour; cook 2 to 3 minutes, then add the clams and chicken stock. Stir continually to activate the flour thickener. Turn heat to low, and simmer uncovered for 30 minutes.

If the chowder is too thick while cooking, add milk in ½-cup increments. During the last 10 minutes of cooking, add the cream and parsley. Taste for salt and pepper. Remove and discard the bay leaf. Spoon the hot chowder into the hollowed-out bread bowls.

Note: I picked up personal-size sourdough bread bowls at my local grocery store's bakery section. I popped them into the oven, sliced off the tops, and hollowed out the excess bread to make room for the chowder.

SOUPS AND STEWS

PREP TIME: 10 minutes COOK TIME: 30–35 minutes YIELD: 4 servings

Taco Soup

INGREDIENTS

1 pound ground chicken

2 tablespoons olive oil

2 quarts chicken stock

1 (15-ounce) can stewed
tomatoes

1 cup brown rice

1 cup dry lentils

1 medium onion, diced (any
color preference)

1 bell pepper, diced

3 ribs celery, diced

1 jalapeño pepper, diced

3 cloves fresh garlic, smashed

1 packet taco seasoning (see
note)

1 teaspoon dried paprika

1 teaspoon garlic powder

1 teaspoon ground turmeric

Salt and pepper to taste

DIRECTIONS

Brown the chicken in the olive oil in a large soup pot. Add the rest of the ingredients. Bring to a simmer, and reduce to low heat.

The soup is done when the rice is done, about 35 minutes. It can get a bit mushy if overcooked.

Note: Seasoning packets are an excellent, cost-effective way to get multiple seasonings without purchasing them individually. Make sure to purchase a packet without additional fillers or chemicals.

PREP TIME: 10 minutes COOK TIME: 30–40 minutes YIELD: 4 servings

Roasted Tomato Soup

INGREDIENTS

2 pounds cherry tomatoes

2 medium yellow onions, chopped

½ cup butter

1 head of garlic, peeled and crushed, about 12 cloves

1 pinch crushed red pepper flakes

Sea salt and pepper to taste

1 quart chicken stock

1 (27-ounce) can San Marzano tomatoes (whole, peeled, in juice or sauce)

1–2 cups heavy cream, to finish

DIRECTIONS

Roast the tomatoes at 425° for 20 minutes, and finish for 1 minute under a high broiler. You want the skins to actually blister.

While the tomatoes are roasting, sauté onions in the butter until soft, about 7 minutes; you don't want them to caramelize, just soften. Add garlic and pepper flakes. Cook for 3 to 4 minutes; do not burn. Season with salt and pepper. Add chicken stock, bring to a boil, and reduce to a simmer.

Once the onions and garlic are soft enough to smash with a spoon, add canned tomatoes and blistered cherry tomatoes: skins, pan juices, and all. Simmer, covered, for 20 to 30 minutes.

Use an immersion blender to blend the soup to your desired thickness. Continue to cook the soup, uncovered, for 10 minutes.

Remove the finished soup from the heat, and swirl in heavy cream and a sprinkle of sea salt. Serve with toasted cheese sandwiches!

SOUPS AND STEWS

PREP TIME: 10 minutes COOK TIME: 25–30 minutes YIELD: 4 servings

Thai Green Curry Soup with Grilled Chicken Skewers

If you want to skip the grilling portion of this recipe, slice the chicken into one-inch cubes and sauté with the onions. This skips a step and tastes just as wonderful. If grilling, wait until after the curry has been made.

INGREDIENTS

1 medium yellow onion, chopped

2 tablespoons olive oil

½ tablespoon green curry paste

4 cups good chicken stock

1 (15-ounce) can coconut milk

2 cups spinach

1 red pepper, thinly sliced

1 zucchini, thinly sliced

½ cup water-packed bamboo shoots, drained (look for these in the Asian foods section of your grocer)

2 cloves fresh garlic, smashed

1 pinch crushed red pepper flakes

For garnish: cilantro, lime wedges, pomegranate seeds, and toasted cashews

CHICKEN SKEWERS

2 boneless, skinless chicken breasts

1 teaspoon oil

1 teaspoon garlic powder

1 teaspoon salt

1 teaspoon pepper

For garnish: cilantro, lime wedges, pomegranate seeds, and toasted cashews

DIRECTIONS

Sauté the onions in the oil and curry paste in a large heavy-bottomed saucepan until soft. Add the rest of the soup ingredients. Simmer everything for about 10 minutes; you want the veggies to still have some bite.

If you are grilling your chicken, take the breast, slice each one into three strips, and place two strips on your grilling skewers.

Rub each skewer with the oil and seasonings. Place them on a hot grill, about 350°, or grill pan, then cook 10 minutes or until the chicken is fully cooked in the center. Serve alongside the soup and enjoy!

Vegetables and Sides

A Best Friend with a Side of Butternut Squash

I was a junior in high school, dressed in my nicest clothing, and I had my ticket! I was getting on a plane all by myself, headed to Flower Mound, Texas, where I would meet up with my very best friend, Jen. But let me back up.

Jennifer and I became friends when I began attending the high school my father had just acquired a teaching position at. She says I had the biggest smile and was very warm when I walked into that math class on my first day. Jen and I hit it off quickly; we were the fastest of friends. I joined school midway through our sophomore year, and Jen's family already had plans to move from Washington State to the great state of Texas. Even though we attended school together for only a few months, I'd never had a friend like her. Everything I did or said was just okay by her. We laughed a lot. We confided in each other. I could be myself completely. Jen was, and is still, so resourceful. She could get into and out of any situation. Once, a few years after she moved to Texas, I showed up to audition for the upcoming revival of *Star Search*. For six hours, I stood in a line with hundreds of other hopeful singers, and I couldn't wait to wow the judges with my rendition of Deanna Carter's "Strawberry Wine." Jen was flying in to be there for me, but time was not on our side; she probably wasn't going to be able to land, grab a car, and make it to the venue before I belted it out before the powers that be. But she was! In spite of time and the heightened security, she was waiting for me, like a miracle, in the judging room! It was unbelievable.

We became pen pals after my dear friend moved away. There were no cell phones in my high school days—even email was relatively new on the scene! So we'd write each other every week and were able to maintain our friendship despite the distance between us. Her father was a commercial pilot, so we were able to see each other often thanks to family flight passes. Either I'd fly down or she'd fly up. She came for homecoming and for my graduation, and that was merely the beginning. Jen goes the distance to be there for all the major moments and big days. She was there when I met the love of my life, and she was there when I opened my restaurant. She was there when I had Noah and also when I had Milo. Jen's been a witness for every tear and has cried along with me. She was my maid of honor, and she saw me off on my honeymoon. She's always good for a ham-and-cheese omelet on a 10:00 p.m. diner run, and she's a travel partner for life! Jen is a big adventure and a tender heart all wrapped up in one beautiful package. She is quiet when I'm loud and supportive when I'm weak, truly the best friend I could ever ask for. We've had our ups and downs and growing pains, for sure, but she is a true-blue clap-when-you-win friend.

So, on that very first visit to her new home in my junior year, her mom made pork chops and butternut squash with this parmesan crust. I had never seen a butternut squash before, let alone one piled with cheese. We sat at the table with her family, and her mom served everyone. I had so many questions about this orange squash. Is it just a Texas squash? "No, Danny!" her mom told me. "They have this in Washington too. Ask your mom to get one. You roast it this way." It was slightly sweet and creamy, and with that cheese on top—delicious. I liked it so much that I was served my own half a squash to enjoy. They seemed charmed by how much I was enjoying it. There was an abundance of grace and joy at that table, a never-ending well of support and love that has followed me all the years since then. Just as there is nothing quite like a best friend, there's nothing quite like a roasted butternut squash with butter and salt and crispy parmesan cheese.

80 VEGETABLES AND SIDES

PREP TIME: 5 minutes COOK TIME: 5 minutes YIELD: 4 servings

Herby Peas

INGREDIENTS

6 thick-cut bacon slices, chopped
2 medium shallots, diced
3 cups frozen peas, thawed
½ cup torn mint
½ cup chopped chives
½ cup chopped fresh dill
4 cups baby spinach
Juice of 1 lemon
Salt and pepper to taste

DIRECTIONS

Brown the bacon and shallots in a skillet over medium-high heat until crisp; add the peas. Stir to deglaze the pan with the moisture from the peas.

Once the peas are hot, add the herbs, and stir gently. Immediately pour the peas, herbs, and bacon fat over the spinach. Add the lemon juice. Add salt and pepper. Gently toss, and serve.

Russelville, Oregon. Great-Uncle Bob, Grandma Gloria, Great-Auntie Charlotte, and Great-Aunt Pat.

VEGETABLES AND SIDES

PREP TIME: 10 minutes COOK TIME: 35 minutes YIELD: 4 servings

Creamy Buttermilk and Parsley Mashed Potatoes

INGREDIENTS

10–12 medium Yukon Gold potatoes

1–2 cups whole milk

1 cup buttermilk

1 cup shredded parmesan cheese

½ cup butter, softened

1 bunch flat parsley, roughly chopped

2 teaspoons kosher salt

DIRECTIONS

Slice potatoes in half, place in a large pan, and cover with cool water. Bring to a boil for 25 to 35 minutes, or until potatoes are tender enough to mash.

Drain water, and add the rest of the ingredients, reserving 1 cup milk to use only if needed. Mash by hand or with a hand mixer.

Taste for salt, and enjoy. The parsley cooks slightly with the heat of the potatoes; these are lovely! Serve alongside Cafeteria Chicken Gravy (page 10).

PREP TIME: 15 minutes COOK TIME: 60 minutes YIELD: 4 servings

Butternut Squash Polenta

INGREDIENTS

1 medium butternut squash

2 teaspoons oil

5 cups chicken stock

1 cup stone-ground cornmeal or polenta

Salt and pepper to taste

1 cup shredded parmesan cheese

½ cup heavy cream

2 tablespoons butter

DIRECTIONS

Preheat the oven to 350°. Slice the squash in half, and scrape out the seeds. Rub with oil, and wrap each half in foil. Place on a baking sheet, and bake for 60 minutes.

Once tender, remove skins, and set flesh aside. Combine the chicken stock and cornmeal in a heavy-bottomed large stockpot. Simmer over medium heat for 45 to 60 minutes, until the cornmeal becomes tender and the liquid is fully absorbed but still loose.

Mash in the roasted butternut squash. Cook for 3–5 additional minutes. Add salt and pepper; taste for seasoning. Remove from heat, and add the cheese, cream, and butter to finish.

PREP TIME: 5 minutes COOK TIME: 5 minutes YIELD: 4 servings

Creamed Spinach

INGREDIENTS

2 pounds (or 10 cups) fresh spinach (yields 2–3 cups of cooked spinach)

1 tablespoon butter

1 clove fresh garlic, smashed

1 cup heavy whipping cream

½ cup shredded parmesan cheese

Salt and pepper to taste

DIRECTIONS

Sauté the spinach in the butter; once it wilts by half, add the garlic. Sauté until the spinach is fully wilted.

Add the cream and cheese; reduce for 2 minutes, until it's bubbly and perfect. Add salt and pepper. Serve alongside a rib eye.

VEGETABLES AND SIDES

PREP TIME: 10 minutes COOK TIME: 45–50 minutes YIELD: 4 servings

Aunty Pat's Dilly Potatoes

I grew up on these potatoes. We'd be having meatloaf or BBQ chicken for dinner, and the moment I walked in from school, I could smell the dill and garlic! My mother made them for company and for church, for special occasions and birthday dinners. These potatoes are my childhood on a plate. I don't think I knew fresh dill existed as a kid, so this is my grown-up, punched-up version of those classic dilly potatoes of my youth, complete with loads of fresh garlic and finished with plenty of fresh dill. My mother's aunt Pat taught her to make these potatoes, and it's likely they were served up in my great-gran Thora's restaurant on top of the Sears Tower in Portland, Oregon, in the sixties. What I wouldn't give to have worked that cook line with my family. What a sight those women must have been, cranking out salads and gravies and smothered *everything*! When I smell the dill and garlic on these baby reds, it delivers a heavy dose of nostalgia and serves as a reminder to keep my head up and work hard, like all the women in my family who came before me.

INGREDIENTS

6 medium-sized Yukon gold or
   red bliss potatoes

2 tablespoons melted butter

2 tablespoons olive oil

6 cloves fresh garlic, roughly
   chopped

2 teaspoons dried dill

1 teaspoon kosher salt

1 teaspoon cracked black
   pepper

½ teaspoon onion powder

1–2 tablespoons chopped fresh
   dill

DIRECTIONS

Preheat the oven to 350°. Slice the potatoes into 6 to 8 wedges per potato, lengthwise. Add all the ingredients except fresh dill to a mixing bowl. Toss to coat the wedges in all that goodness. Pour the contents of the bowl into a 9-by-13-inch baking dish and cover with foil. Bake covered for 20 minutes. Remove the foil and bake until the potatoes are tender and a crisp, golden brown. Garnish with fresh dill.

Roasted Carrots with Cilantro Yogurt

PREP TIME: 10 minutes COOK TIME: 20 minutes YIELD: 4 servings

Roasted Carrots with Cilantro Yogurt

INGREDIENTS

2 bunches fresh carrots, greens
   trimmed but about 1 inch of
   the tops left on
2 tablespoons olive oil
Salt and pepper to taste

CILANTRO YOGURT

1 cup full-fat, plain Greek
   yogurt
½ cup chopped cilantro
2 tablespoons olive oil
1 clove fresh garlic
Salt and pepper to taste
½ cup toasted, chopped
   pistachios for garnish

DIRECTIONS

Preheat the oven to 375°. Toss trimmed carrots in olive oil and
salt and pepper, and roast for 20 minutes. Put all the ingredients
for the yogurt in a food processor, and pulse 3 to 4 times.

Pour the yogurt onto a platter, and put the warm carrots on top.
Sprinkle toasted, chopped pistachios on top.

PREP TIME: 5 minutes COOK TIME: 10 minutes YIELD: 4 servings

Garlic and Brown Butter Asparagus

INGREDIENTS

1 pound fresh asparagus, woody ends trimmed
2 tablespoons butter
4 cloves fresh garlic, minced
Salt and pepper to taste

DIRECTIONS

Steam the asparagus in a skillet on medium-high heat for 3 minutes. Drain the excess water, remove the asparagus, and add the butter to the pan.

Once the butter starts to foam and turn brown (it will smell fragrant and almost nutty), add the garlic. Let it bubble and spatter for about 30 seconds.

Return asparagus to the pan, and toss in the butter to coat the spears. Add salt and pepper.

The Gresham Farm, Oregon. Great-Uncle Dick and Great-Uncle Russ.

PREP TIME: 5 minutes COOK TIME: 35 minutes YIELD: 4 servings

Roasted Butternut Squash with Parmesan Cheese

My very best friend in the whole wide world just happens to live in Texas. We've stayed friends for twenty years, since we were sophomores in high school. We've flown all over the world and have been on so many hilarious vacations. She's been in my life for the good, the bad, and the ugly. This dish doesn't represent her at all, but it's funny: I think of her every time I make it. Her mother introduced me to butternut squash. I had never even seen one until I was eighteen, and her mother made us one for dinner. She roasted it and sprinkled parmesan cheese on it, and I was in love! Roasted squash was an entirely new thing for me.

INGREDIENTS

1 medium butternut squash, sliced lengthwise, seeds removed

1 teaspoon olive oil

Salt and pepper to taste

½ cup grated parmesan cheese

DIRECTIONS

Preheat the oven to 375°. Rub the inside of each side of the squash with olive oil. Salt and pepper the squash. Lay it flesh-side down on a baking sheet. Bake for 35 minutes, until it's fork tender.

Flip the squash over, sprinkle with the parmesan cheese, and pop under the broiler for 2 minutes to melt and bubble the cheese.

Remove from the oven, and let stand 5 minutes before serving.

VEGETABLES AND SIDES 91

PREP TIME: 10 minutes COOK TIME: 45 minutes YIELD: 4 servings

Easter Potatoes with Feta, Cream Cheese, and Dill

I can still see my great-uncle Bill standing over a large wooden bowl, mixing up a massive Caesar salad with tiny Oregon bay shrimp and our favorite dressing—extra lemon and croutons on mine, please. I was ten years old, and it was my favorite thing ever to watch him mix that salad. I love my great-uncle Bill: gray hair and big glasses, hugs for days, and a big "Oh, I love you, Danny."

It's Easter Sunday: egg hunts and a new dress, and Easter dinner at my grandma Gloria's house. The nostalgia of our childhood is a powerful thing. I think back on this time often in the spring, and I can't help but smile. I felt like a princess in my new dress. Church seemed so much more special on Easter. Even as a child, I knew the significance.

I anticipated the Easter holiday for months. When we were kids, my mom would get my sister and me a new dress for church, and I can remember putting it on and feeling brand-new, special. I can't help but think that's really what it's all about. Jesus came and died specifically for our sins, so that we might live a new life: something brand-new. The thought of our savior's love and sacrifice for us during this special time means that we get a chance at a happy life, an abundant life filled with joy. Not without trial or pain, but fresh and beautiful nonetheless.

My prayer for you and your family during this sweet time is that you spend more time together, and less time worrying: more time at family dinner, and less time scrambling just to get by. If we let it, life can run us. We often forget we call the shots. I hope you call some quiet rest into your life and really take in all the spring has to offer: cherry blossoms and the first cut grass of the season. Crocus and tulips and sugar snap peas. Jesus died so that we might live abundantly. By golly, I'm gonna LIVE!!!

This pretty darn simple spin on this Easter side dish is one of my favorites, with some deliciously tasty twists. Go ahead and make every bit of it.

CONTINUED

Easter Potatoes with Feta, Cream Cheese, and Dill

INGREDIENTS

8–10 medium Yukon Gold
   potatoes

1 tablespoon butter

1 yellow onion, sliced

3 cloves fresh garlic, chopped

8 ounces cream cheese,
   softened

Salt and pepper to taste

3 cups heavy cream

½ cup milk

1 tablespoon all-purpose flour

¾ cup crumbled feta cheese,
   plus 2 tablespoons set aside

½ cup chopped fresh dill, plus
   2 tablespoons set aside

DIRECTIONS

Bring potatoes to a boil in a large pot of salted water for 15
to 20 minutes, until knife tender but not completely cooked
through. Drain, rinse, and set aside to cool while you make the
cream-cheese mixture.

Preheat the oven to 350°. Cook the onions in the butter in a
large sauté or saucepan over medium heat until translucent,
then add the garlic and sauté 2 minutes more, until the garlic is
tender.

Melt the cream cheese completely into the onion and garlic; add
salt and pepper. Add cream and milk. Cook for 1 to 2 minutes,
stirring often, until everything begins to come together.

Sprinkle flour over the mixture, stir to combine, and cook
for 1 to 2 minutes, then add feta cheese and fresh dill. Stir to
incorporate.

Slice or dice potatoes, whichever you prefer, and lay them in a
9-by-13-inch pan. Pour the hot cream-cheese mixture over the
potatoes, sprinkle with the 2 tablespoons of set-aside feta, and
bake uncovered for 15 to 20 minutes, until the top begins to
turn light golden brown.

Once the potatoes are cooked perfectly, remove from the oven,
and sprinkle with the remaining fresh dill. A squeeze of lemon
to finish the dish is lovely but optional.

PREP TIME: 5 minutes COOK TIME: 35 minutes YIELD: 4 servings

Roasted Cauliflower and Capers

INGREDIENTS

1 head cauliflower, sliced into bite-size florets

1 red onion, sliced

½ cup capers, rinsed and drained

½ cup grated parmesan cheese

2 tablespoons olive oil

Salt and pepper to taste

Woodsy herbs such as thyme or rosemary (optional; they work well in this)

DIRECTIONS

Preheat the oven to 350°. Line a baking sheet with parchment paper. Simply toss everything together, and bake until caramelized and tender, about 35 minutes.

Gresham, Oregon. Auntie Ingrid and Uncle Telvin's dairy farm.

VEGETABLES AND SIDES 95

PREP TIME: 5 minutes COOK TIME: 5 minutes YIELD: 4 servings

Off-the-Cob Street Corn with Chipotle and Feta

INGREDIENTS

5 ears fresh corn

2 tablespoons butter

1 chipotle pepper, chopped

½ cup chopped cilantro

½ cup crumbled feta cheese

Salt and pepper to taste

Juice of 2 limes

DIRECTIONS

Slice the corn off the cob using the two-bowl method: Place a small bowl upside down inside a large mixing bowl, and stand the corn on the smaller bowl's bottom to slice off the kernels. The corn will fall nicely into the bowl.

Sauté the corn for 3 to 5 minutes over medium heat in the melted butter.

Add the chopped chipotle pepper, cilantro, and cheese. Add salt and pepper. Add the lime juice. Toss to mix, and enjoy!

VEGETABLES AND SIDES

PREP TIME: 15 minutes COOK TIME: 12 minutes YIELD: 4 servings

Kale and Fresh Crab Caesar Salad with Pepita Caesar Dressing

SALAD

1 bunch your favorite kale, torn and ribs removed

1 head red leaf lettuce, chopped

¾ cup pomegranate seeds

½ cup toasted pepita seeds

2 cups Herbed Croutons (recipe follows)

1 pound fresh Dungeness crab

1 cup Pepita Caesar Dressing (recipe follows)

PEPITA CAESAR DRESSING

¾ cup olive oil

2 tablespoons Dijon mustard

2 tablespoons toasted pepita seeds

2 anchovy filets packed in oil

Juice of 2 Meyer lemons

Juice of 1 mandarin orange

Salt and cracked pepper to taste

1 pinch crushed red pepper flakes (optional)

HERBED CROUTONS

5 slices artisan country bread, cubed

½ cup melted butter

¼ cup chopped Italian parsley

3 tablespoons olive oil

2 tablespoons fresh lemon thyme leaves

Salt and fresh cracked pepper to taste

FOR THE SALAD

Layer the ingredients for the salad in the order they appear in a large serving bowl or platter. Drizzle at least 1 cup of the Pepita Caesar Dressing over the top, and serve. If you'd like the kale wilted, dress it and set it aside in the refrigerator up to 2 hours before assembling the salad.

FOR THE DRESSING

Pulse all the ingredients in a food processor. Dressing keeps for up to 1 week.

FOR THE HERBED CROUTONS

Preheat the oven on the convection setting to 375°. Combine all the ingredients in a mixing bowl, and gently toss to coat each bread cube in the butter, oil, herbs, and seasonings. Arrange croutons on a lined baking sheet, and bake for 10 to 12 minutes. Stir the croutons halfway through baking to ensure they don't burn and that they brown evenly.

PREP TIME: 5 minutes COOK TIME: 10 minutes YIELD: 4 servings

Peas and Orzo

INGREDIENTS

8–10 ounces dry orzo pasta

1 cup frozen peas

½ cup fresh chopped basil

½ cup fresh chopped Italian
  parsley

DRESSING

1 cup finely grated parmesan
  cheese

½ cup champagne vinegar

½ cup olive oil

¼ cup Dijon mustard

Juice and zest of 1 lemon

1 clove fresh garlic, smashed
  but whole

1 tablespoon honey

Salt and pepper to taste

DIRECTIONS

Cook the orzo according to directions on the package. Drain, and add to a large mixing bowl. Add frozen peas and herbs to the hot pasta.

Whisk together all the ingredients for the dressing, and pour it over the pasta, peas, basil, and parsley; mix to gently combine, and refrigerate 30 minutes before serving.

VEGETABLES AND SIDES 101

Everyday Green Salad

PREP TIME: 10 minutes **YIELD:** 4 servings

Everyday Green Salad

INGREDIENTS

2 heads butter or Boston lettuce
(about 5–6 cups)

1 cup crumbled sharp white
cheddar cheese

1 cup toasted walnuts

1 firm pear, thinly sliced into
matchsticks

CLASSIC CITRUS VINAIGRETTE

2 tablespoons finely diced
onions

Juice and zest of one lemon

½ cup light tasting oil

1 tablespoon white or
champagne vinegar

1 teaspoon honey

½ teaspoon kosher salt

¼ teaspoon freshly cracked
black pepper

DIRECTIONS

Wash and tear the lettuce into large pieces and place in a large serving bowl. Sprinkle the cheese, walnuts, and pear over top of the lettuce, and set aside.

To prepare the dressing, allow the onion to sit in the lemon juice and vinegar for at least 3 to 4 minutes before whisking in the rest of the ingredients.

Pour the desired amount of dressing over top of the greens and gently mix before serving.

PREP TIME: 10 minutes COOK TIME: 20 minutes YIELD: 4 servings

Thora's Steakhouse Crispy Onion Rings with Buttermilk Ranch Dipping Sauce

I like to mix the ranch ingredients in a medium-sized bowl first and set it in the fridge while I'm making everything else so it has time to come together.

CRISPY ONION RINGS

3 peeled onions, sliced ¼-inch thick, thinner if you can

1 cup buttermilk (reserve ¼ cup after onions have soaked)

6 cups oil, suitable for frying

2 cups all-purpose flour

2 tablespoons cornstarch

2 teaspoons kosher salt

1 teaspoon cracked black pepper

1 teaspoon garlic powder

½ teaspoon ground cayenne pepper

BUTTERMILK RANCH DIPPING SAUCE

1 cup sour cream

¼ cup buttermilk the onions soaked in

2 tablespoons chopped fresh chives

1 teaspoon garlic powder

1 teaspoon kosher salt

½ teaspoon black pepper

½ teaspoon dried thyme

½ teaspoon dried rosemary

DIRECTIONS

For the crispy onion rings, pour buttermilk over onions, and let them stand at room temperature while you prepare the oil.

Bring the oil to 300° in a large heatproof pot. (If you don't have a thermometer, that's fine; it'll begin to shimmer and appear like it's moving.) Don't let the oil smoke.

Whisk the flour, cornstarch, and seasonings together. Dip the soaked onions into the seasoned flour, shake off the excess, and drop the onions into the oil. You'll need to work quickly and in batches.

Fry the onions until they are golden brown. Drain on a plate with paper towels. Sprinkle a little extra kosher salt over the fried onion rings. Dip these beauties into the buttermilk dressing or serve with a fun meal.

PREP TIME: 10 minutes YIELD: 4 servings

Tomato and Cucumber Salad

During the summer, I don't think we had a meal without this simple and flavorful salad. It's a cheap way to use up all the end-of-summer produce. My mom used a bottle of Italian dressing, but I figured out a method that is even tastier and skips the packaged food.

INGREDIENTS

1 English cucumber, sliced into rounds

1 cup cherry tomatoes, sliced in half

½ red onion, sliced as thinly as you can (see note)

DRESSING

½ cup olive oil

½ cup finely grated parmesan cheese (see note)

2 tablespoons lemon juice

1 tablespoon champagne vinegar

2 teaspoons dry oregano

1 clove fresh garlic, crushed

1 teaspoon honey

Salt and pepper to taste

DIRECTIONS

Mix the dressing first by combining all the ingredients, then simply toss the cucumber, tomatoes, and onions with it. Discard the garlic clove, as you want only the fresh garlic essence.

Note: If you soak the sliced onions in water for 10 minutes and drain them well, they will lose that unpleasant, pungent onion bite. I give my hunk of shredded parm a quick whirl in the food processor, and it creates a fine grate that is perfect for dressings and dips.

PREP TIME: 5 minutes **COOK TIME:** 15–20 minutes **YIELD:** 4 servings

Cream Cheese Polenta

INGREDIENTS

3–4 cups water or low-sodium chicken stock

1 cup yellow corn grits or medium-grind cornmeal (see note)

2 tablespoons butter

8 ounces cream cheese, softened

1 cup shredded parmesan cheese

Milk, as needed

Salt and pepper to taste

DIRECTIONS

Bring the water and grits or cornmeal to a boil in a medium saucepan, then reduce heat to low. Cook until the grits become tender and absorb the water, stirring constantly. (If it looks dry, add more water or stock.)

Melt the butter into the grits, and stir in the cream cheese and parmesan. The polenta should be soft and creamy (this whole process takes about 15 minutes). Add milk or stock to thin.

Note: Cooking time varies greatly, depending on the style of grits/polenta you buy. I love the quick-cooking brands that are whole grain and non-GMO. Cornmeal works but not as nicely; you want the larger grind for good texture. The old-fashioned or long-cooking kind can take up to 30 minutes and needs a great deal more liquid. Bob's Red Mill polenta is my favorite brand.

Roasted Radishes

PREP TIME: 5 minutes COOK TIME: 35 minutes YIELD: 4 servings

Roasted Radishes

This hardly feels like a recipe, but it's so lovely and unexpected. Radishes are a root like any other but with a higher water content.

INGREDIENTS

2–3 bunches red, crunchy radishes, greens trimmed off

2 tablespoons olive oil

Salt and pepper to taste

DIRECTIONS

Simply trim the radishes and slice in half lengthwise. Line a baking sheet with parchment paper. Toss the trimmed roots with olive oil, salt, and pepper, and place in the oven for 25 to 35 minutes, until they have caramelized and roasted to perfection.

PREP TIME: 5 minutes COOK TIME: 20 minutes YIELD: 4 servings

Spring Potatoes

INGREDIENTS

1 pound tiny new potatoes

2 tablespoons olive oil

Salt and pepper to taste

1 medium onion, sliced (any color preferred)

2 tablespoons butter

1 cup fresh sugar peas, hulled

DIRECTIONS

Preheat the oven to 375°. Parboil the potatoes by covering them with water, and bring to a boil for 10 minutes; drain, and slice the potatoes in half.

Cover the spuds in the olive oil and salt and pepper, and bake for 15 to 20 minutes on a parchment-lined baking sheet.

Meanwhile, caramelize the onion in the butter over medium heat. Add the peas at the very end, and toss in the crispy potatoes.

VEGETABLES AND SIDES 109

PREP TIME: 5 minutes COOK TIME: 5 minutes YIELD: 4 servings

Jenny's Perfectly Steamed Broccoli and Cauliflower

This recipe is almost too easy to write, but I know no one likes a mushy veggie. My sister, Jenny, is always in charge of the perfectly steamed veggies, and this method is guaranteed to work every time.

INGREDIENTS

2 cups broccoli florets

2 cups cauliflower florets

4 cups water

2 teaspoons salt

¼ cup butter

DIRECTIONS

Bring the water to a boil, add the veggies, cover with a lid, and set a timer for 5 minutes. Drain the water, and toss the veggies in the salt and butter. Sauté on medium-high heat for about a minute or so to melt the butter, and you're set.

PREP TIME: 10 minutes COOK TIME: 60 minutes YIELD: 4–6 servings

Mom's Scalloped Potatoes

INGREDIENTS

6 white or gold potatoes, peeled and sliced

½ medium onion, finely diced (any color preferred)

1 pound button mushrooms, finely diced

4–6 slices uncured bacon, or 1 cup diced ham

¼ cup butter

¼ cup all-purpose flour

Salt and pepper to taste

6 cups milk

2 cups shredded sharp cheddar cheese

1 cup grated parmesan cheese

DIRECTIONS

Preheat the oven to 300°. Cover the potatoes with water and bring to a boil, then reduce to a simmer for 30 minutes or until potatoes are tender but not falling apart.

Sauté the onion, mushrooms, and bacon in the butter until the bacon is rendered and fully cooked. Add the flour to create a roux. Cook the flour for 3 to 5 minutes, until the roux begins to bubble and spatter. Season with plenty of salt and pepper.

Slowly add the milk, and bring to a simmer. Once the sauce has thickened, remove from heat and add the cheeses.

Generously butter a 9-by-13-inch pan, and add the sliced potatoes. Pour the creamy sauce over top and cover with foil. Bake for 30 minutes. If desired, sprinkle extra cheese over the top to finish.

VEGETABLES AND SIDES 111

Old-Fashioned Dill and Mustard Potato Salad

PREP TIME: 5 minutes COOK TIME: 30 minutes, inactive 2–4 hours
YIELD: 4–6 servings

Old-Fashioned Dill and Mustard Potato Salad

My mom tells us a story about our great-gran Thora, the cooking matriarch of the family, who has passed. On my mother's wedding day, when she was all of seventeen years old, my great-grandma heard there wasn't going to be food—just cake and coffee. She decided that was not acceptable. She purchased everything to make a country-style feast, with a baked ham and potato salad for everyone at the wedding. Early into her marriage, my mother was trying to make the salad, and it just didn't turn out. She called Thora, who said to never use Miracle Whip, only good mayonnaise. The mystery was solved. I hope you love this as much as we do; it's quite possibly the most delicious salad you'll ever bring to any picnic. The secret's in the pickle juice!

INGREDIENTS

5 white or gold potatoes, peeled
6 eggs, room temperature, shell on
1 cup diced dill pickle
1 cup mayonnaise
½ cup chopped fresh dill
½ cup yellow mustard
¼ cup pickle juice (from the jar)
1 rib celery, diced
¼ white onion, grated

DIRECTIONS

Cover the potatoes with water, and bring to a boil; this will take about 30 minutes. Add the eggs with 10 minutes of cooking time to go. Dice the potatoes and eggs, and put them in a large mixing bowl. You want the potatoes just cooked; overcooked potatoes will get too mushy. Add all the remaining ingredients, mix gently, and taste for salt and pepper. Refrigerate for 2 to 4 hours before serving.

Tacoma, Washington. Great-Gran Thora and my mother, Dianna, on her wedding day.

VEGETABLES AND SIDES   113

PREP TIME: 5 minutes COOK TIME: 35 minutes YIELD: 4 servings

Roasted Winter Vegetables

INGREDIENTS

7–8 carrots

6–7 radishes

3 parsnips

3 medium shallots

⅛ cup olive oil, suitable for roasting

1½ teaspoons kosher salt

1 teaspoon cracked black pepper

5 sprigs thyme

DIRECTIONS

Preheat the oven to 375°. Slice the carrots and the rest of the vegetables lengthwise (some pieces might need to be sliced in half again, but don't be afraid of big, chunky veggies).

Arrange the sliced vegetables on a parchment-lined baking sheet, and coat in olive oil.

Sprinkle salt and pepper over top, then scatter the thyme around the pan. Bake for at least 35 minutes. You want the vegetables tender and caramelized!

Snacks

Life Happens In Between

Snacks: the food we eat in between our meals, the food we grab on the go, the little bits eaten before bed with tiny hands reaching up for just another bite. Breakfast, lunch, and dinner are what we set our clocks by and what we nourish our bodies with during the day. We plan them, we look forward to them, and when it comes to feeding our families, meals get all the attention. Yeah, they're important. But who doesn't pause for a snack every now and again? Snacks aren't typically planned or given much consideration beforehand. But they're important. They happen in between. I think life is like this.

Oftentimes, we associate happiness or success with the big moments of our lives. It's true that nothing quite holds a candle to our weddings, the days our babies are born, or the big promotion you've been working toward, the job you landed that took *years*. All these moments are worth celebrating, of course. But the in-between, lesser-celebrated moments are the backbone of our lives. I mean those times driving in your car, head bopping to your favorite song, standing in the line at the grocery store, or waving hello to a stranger.

Sometimes, these in-between moments transform themselves into more meaningful ones. I was traveling through Nashville recently, and a man was just behind me laughing and chatting away on his phone in the security line. You know how some people command attention just by *being*? He was one of those fellows: big smile, warm demeanor. I sent my belongings through the X-ray machine and zipped on through. When I sat to put my shoes back on, I noticed a woman sharing my bench and the man with the big smile standing nearby; they were clearly traveling together. But now his lips drew downward and he wore a look of shock and sadness on his face. He held his shoes in one hand and looked at his phone in the other.

Not noticing this shift in his demeanor, she smiled, stood, and said, "Well, are you ready, slowpoke?"

He stared at her blankly.

"Are you okay?" she said, concerned.

Very quietly, he said, "My daddy died."

She stood there, stunned and sad. "I'm so, so sorry."

He stepped away for privacy and tried to collect himself. I'd never met this man in my life. It took all kinds of courage to approach him. I walked up to him, sweat beginning to collect on my brow. Approaching a man in his time of grief is a big deal.

"Sir," I said, "I'm so sorry. I overheard that you've just lost your father. Can I pray for you?"

He looked at me in disbelief. "Why, yes," he said, "I think you can." He wrapped me in a huge embrace and began to cry as I prayed for comfort, for peace, and thanked the Lord for his dad's life. Afterward, as I stepped away, he said thank you. And then we parted ways.

Approaching that gentleman during his difficult time was one of the toughest things I may have ever done, and the situation arose in the midst of an in-between moment, just maneuvering through airport security. But this moment was truly important work. It was honest living without recognition or praise. I think that life's in-between moments are a cause for celebration because that's where real living happens.

White Cheddar Toast with Dill and Tomatoes

PREP TIME: 10 minutes COOK TIME: 7–8 minutes YIELD: 4 servings

White Cheddar Toast with Dill and Tomatoes

INGREDIENTS

2 cups cherry tomatoes, halved

1 clove fresh garlic, smashed
   and diced

⅓ cup olive oil

½ cup chopped fresh baby dill

Salt and pepper to taste

6 slices artisan country-style
   bread

2 cups shredded sharp white
   cheddar cheese

DIRECTIONS

Preheat the oven to 350°. Mix the tomatoes, garlic, oil, herbs, and seasonings, and set aside to marinate.

Load each slice of bread with roughly ⅓ cup of the cheese, and bake until melted and just beginning to bubble.

Spoon tomato mixture over the top of each warm slice of cheesy toast.

PREP TIME: 10 minutes COOK TIME: 40 minutes YIELD: 4–6 servings

Homestyle Garlic Fries

INGREDIENTS

8 medium Yukon Gold potatoes,
  sliced into wedges
¼ cup olive oil, suitable for
  baking
Salt and pepper to taste
10 cloves fresh garlic, chopped
2 tablespoons butter
½ cup chopped parsley

DIRECTIONS

Preheat the oven to 350°. Arrange the potatoes on a large baking sheet, and drizzle with oil. Use your hands to spread the oil evenly over every potato wedge. Salt and pepper liberally. Bake for 30 to 40 minutes, or until the potatoes are golden on the outside and tender with a knife test.

Meanwhile, sauté the garlic in the butter over medium heat. Cook for 2 to 3 minutes, stirring constantly, then add parsley.

When the potatoes are finished, sprinkle the hot garlic mixture over the top. Mix with tongs to evenly coat each wedge. Serve immediately.

PREP TIME: 25 minutes COOK TIME: inactive 3–4 weeks in fridge
YIELD: 1 pint

Pickles

This recipe works for all kinds of veggies: string beans, carrots, even hot peppers. I pickle everything in September; it's back-to-school time and the end of the jam season. I am always trying to squeeze out every last drop of summer to last us until next year. Every year, I make at least ten to fifteen quarts and give them away to my friends and family to store in their fridges. These pickles are easy and perfect each and every year; I have never had a bad batch. You can stuff the jars with large slices of cucumbers and make big spears for a fun variety of shapes and textures.

INGREDIENTS

1 stalk fresh dill, wound into a circle

3–4 cloves garlic, peeled

3 teaspoons pickling salt

2 teaspoons mustard seeds

15 whole black peppercorns

1 dried red chili pepper

¼ teaspoon alum

¼ fresh jalapeño

1 slice sweet red bell pepper, placed inside the wall of a jar

5 medium pickling cucumbers, blossom ends removed

2–3 small pickling cucumbers, blossom ends removed

½ cup apple cider vinegar with at least 5% acidity

DIRECTIONS

Add the ingredients in order to a 1-pint jar.

Fill each jar with tap water to within ½ inch of the rim. Place clean, fresh lid on top, and screw it down to secure. Shake each jar gently to dissolve powders.

Store in the refrigerator; pickles will be ready to eat in 3 to 4 weeks and will last up to 6 months.

SNACKS 125

PREP TIME: 5 minutes COOK TIME: 10 minutes YIELD: 4 servings

Rosemary and Parmesan Popcorn

INGREDIENTS

2 sprigs fresh rosemary,
   chopped and divided

½ cup grated parmesan cheese

3 tablespoons oil, suitable for
   high-temp cooking

½ cup popcorn kernels

2 tablespoons butter, melted

½ teaspoon cracked black
   pepper

DIRECTIONS

Mix 1 teaspoon rosemary with the parmesan cheese, and set aside. Heat the oil, the rest of the rosemary, and the popcorn kernels in a large, lidded pot over medium heat. The kernels will start to pop rapidly; once they slow, pull the pot from the heat.

While the popcorn is still hot, transfer it to a serving bowl, drizzle on butter, and sprinkle on the rosemary-cheese mixture. Season with pepper to taste.

PREP TIME: 5 minutes COOK TIME: 40 minutes YIELD: 4 servings

Spicy Sweet Potato Fries with Sun-Dried Tomato Mayo

INGREDIENTS

3 medium sweet potatoes (see note)
2 tablespoons olive oil
1 teaspoon freshly ground black pepper
1 teaspoon chili powder
1 teaspoon garlic powder
1 teaspoon salt

SUN-DRIED TOMATO MAYO

1 cup mayo
½ cup grated parmesan cheese
½ cup sun-dried tomatoes, packed in oil
½ teaspoon garlic powder
¼ teaspoon freshly ground black pepper
1 pinch salt

DIRECTIONS

Preheat the oven to 350°. Line a baking sheet with parchment paper; set aside.

Slice the sweet potatoes to resemble french fries, about ½-inch thick. Mix the potatoes, oil, and seasonings in a large bowl. Take care to cover each slice of potato with the oil and seasonings. Dump the seasoned potatoes onto the baking sheet. Bake for 30 to 40 minutes, flipping the fries halfway through.

To make the mayo, buzz it all in your food processor, and dunk the hot fries into the goodness!

Note: Sweet potatoes have a higher sugar content than regular potatoes and can burn easily. Watch them for overcooking. Crack the oven door or take them out sooner, depending on how thinly they're sliced.

PREP TIME: 15 minutes COOK TIME: 20 minutes YIELD: 4 servings

Buttermilk Fried Oysters and Razor Clams

INGREDIENTS

1 pound fresh razor clams, sliced in strips (if available; if not, oysters alone work beautifully)

1 pound fresh small oysters

1 cup buttermilk

1 cup all-purpose flour

1 cup superfine cornmeal

2 teaspoons kosher salt

1 teaspoon freshly cracked black pepper

1 teaspoon ground paprika

1 teaspoon garlic powder

1 teaspoon onion powder

½ teaspoon ground cayenne pepper

2 cups light-tasting oil, suitable for shallow frying, like grapeseed or canola

Sea salt and lemon, for serving (optional)

LEMON DILL AIOLI

1 cup mayo

Juice and zest of ½ a lemon

2 tablespoons chopped fresh dill

½ clove fresh garlic, crushed

Salt and pepper to taste

DIRECTIONS

Pour the buttermilk over the clams and oysters in a large mixing bowl. In a separate bowl, mix all the dry ingredients to form a dredge.

Place the oil in a frying pan, and heat it over medium heat until shimmering hot. Dredge the buttermilk-soaked oysters and clams through the flour mixture. Coat evenly, shake off the excess flour, and lay 7 to 10 oysters and clams in the hot oil. Do not overcrowd the pan.

Turn oysters and clams once after 2 to 3 minutes or once they've achieved a golden-brown crust, and continue cooking for another 2 minutes.

Lay finished oysters on a plate lined with paper towels. It should take no more than 5 or 6 minutes to cook each batch.

Sprinkle finished oysters with sea salt and a squeeze of lemon. Serve with Lemon Dill Aioli.

FOR THE LEMON DILL AIOLI

Mix all the ingredients in a bowl, and enjoy! It keeps up to 3 days in the fridge.

SNACKS 129

Caramelized Brie and Tomatoes

PREP TIME: 5 minutes COOK TIME: 7–10 minutes YIELD: 4–6 servings

Caramelized Brie and Tomatoes

INGREDIENTS

1 wheel Brie, any size that suits your needs

1 cup halved cherry tomatoes

Fresh woodsy herbs, like lemon thyme or rosemary

Splash aged balsamic vinegar

DIRECTIONS

This is more of a method than anything. I like to gently slice the top skin off a wheel of Brie; top it with the tomatoes, herbs, and vinegar; and broil for 3 to 5 minutes, until the tomatoes blister and the Brie is melty and perfect for smearing on bread. Be very careful, and watch this closely. The tomatoes might burn, and the Brie might separate if it's kept in the oven too long.

Great Falls, Montana. Grandma Gloria, Great-Auntie Charlotte, and Great-Aunt Pat near Great-Grandpa Danielson's meat truck.

SNACKS 131

Breakfast

Pancakes and Hope

Sometimes, you just have to pull over. You have to make it past all your insecurities and stuff all your fears deep down into your belly and move forward. You need to make a difference in people's lives and say what you are really thinking.

It was Mother's Day, and Mama (me) likes a fancy breakfast. I like eggs Benedict with fresh herbs and extra-lemony hollandaise. I like avocado toast loaded with chili flakes, microgreens, and homemade dill oil. Daddy and Noah like stick-to-your-ribs chocolate-chip pancakes and Denver scrambles from greasy spoons. Because I am a generous gal, and I can make a poached egg any old day, I felt like *Hey! It's Mother's Day, and I am not cooking; you boys choose where we go.* Mike picked in an instant and said, "Babe, you sure? We can go get a frilly breakfast for you—it's Mother's Day!" I was sure. I just wanted to be with my family and not particularly at the stove.

It was 8:00 a.m., and we rolled into the diner like a troop of disheveled lumps ready for breakfast. We ordered two sausage skillets with potatoes and eggs, chocolate-chip pancakes, strong coffee, and freshly squeezed tangerine juice, with an extra side of sausage. We sat quietly, enjoying the older crowd and young families that surrounded us on such an early outing. I knew we had to eat early to avoid a rush.

Our waitress poured our coffee as another sat a group of older gentlemen next to us. These men looked established, well-dressed, and handsome, but I thought it odd they had no ladies or family with them on Mother's Day. They gave each other robust handshakes and loving hugs as they greeted one another. As they ordered their coffee, I couldn't help but overhear their conversation. One man talked about the loneliness he felt after his divorce and how his life had unfolded. Now in his late sixties, he asked his comrades, "What is this life for?"

Our breakfast came, and Noah was thrilled. I cut up his pancakes, and as I sneaked a bite, I was drawn back into listening to the men next to us.

Michael said, "Babe, are you listening?"

I said, "Yes. Can you hear? It's sort of heartbreaking." The men continued, and two of them tried to console their friend as he talked of loss and sobriety and the mistakes he made that left him empty. He spoke of divorce and his children and how he had all the money in the world but no happiness. He said there was an intense void he was feeling, approaching what were always meant to be the happiest years, but he felt no such thing. The other men tried their best to cheer him up, but I found their advice quite empty: Get a puppy or a hobby; go on a vacation!

We finished our breakfast, paid our bill, and walked to our car. I leaned into Mike and said, "I should tell that man that his life wasn't a mistake, that he has a purpose."

Mike said, "Oh, no. It's okay. I'm sure he will be fine." We got into our car, and I said I felt like he needed someone to tell him that life is generally one big mistake, but the void he was feeling was meant to be filled with hope and that God loves him.

Just as we turned out of the parking lot and onto the busy street, I saw the three men exit the diner. I yelled at Mike, "Turn around!"

He said, "Really?"

I said yes.

Noah was echoing my demands, chanting, "Turn around! Turn around!" We whipped right back in, and I saw the man sitting in his truck, gathering himself to drive away. I jumped out of my car and tapped on the passenger-side window.

He rolled it down with hesitation but asked, "Can I help you?" This is where I had forgotten what I looked like: disheveled and in need of a shower. I had forgotten that my car needed a wash, and there was stuff piled up in the windows. What happened next, I could not have prepared for. When things happen that change our lives and shake our very core, we rarely plan for them. These events are gifts that we need to be open to, ready for the possibility.

I said to him, "I am sorry to bother you, sir, but I couldn't help but overhear your conversation at breakfast today. You spoke of a void and an emptiness. You spoke of feeling no hope. I just felt like I had to tell you that your life isn't a giant mistake, that God hasn't forgotten you, and that you have a purpose as long as there

Noah and me.

is breath in your lungs. Whatever mistakes you've made in your past…well, it's okay; that was the past."

I paused, and my heart beat as if it were about to leap out of my chest. I saw tears fill his eyes. His lips quivered as he replied, "Thank you."

I continued. "I hope you don't find me crazy, but I know you needed to know: that void in your heart is God-shaped. Fill it with Him, and you'll be okay." He stared deeply into my eyes, and there was a pause of calm while tears stained his cheeks.

I turned to get back in our car, and as I climbed in, Noah said, "Mama, what did you tell that man?"

I said, "Honey, that God loves him, and he's not forgotten."

"Oh, that's good, Mama," he said. "Did we save my pancake? I want to eat it." We had saved his pancake.

I smiled, and my heart was full. Sometimes we need to jump far out of our comfort zones in order to not only impact others' lives but change our own. I am so happy Noah got to witness the entire event; it was the best Mother's Day present I could have asked for.

Today, turn the car around, jump out, and do that thing you didn't quite think you had the guts to do.

PREP TIME: 5 minutes COOK TIME: 15–20 minutes
YIELD: 10–12 pancakes

Cinnamon Vanilla Ricotta Pancakes

INGREDIENTS

3 eggs, separated

1½ cups half-and-half

1 cup fresh ricotta cheese

2 teaspoons vanilla extract

2 cups all-purpose flour,
    spooned and leveled

1 tablespoon baking powder

½ teaspoon kosher salt

1 teaspoon cinnamon

Butter for the skillet

DIRECTIONS

Whisk the egg whites to stiff peaks, and set aside. Combine the remaining wet ingredients, including the egg yolks, until thoroughly mixed. Add the flour, baking powder, salt, and cinnamon, and gently mix.

Add half the beaten egg whites to the batter, and gently fold from the center out, giving the bowl a quarter turn after each fold. Add the remaining egg whites, and repeat the crosscut mixing until it's just combined.

Heat and butter a nonstick skillet over medium heat. Pour ½-cup ladles of the batter into the warm pan. Wait for bubbles to appear on top of the pancake, and flip. Cook an additional 2 minutes.

136 BREAKFAST

PREP TIME: 10 minutes COOK TIME: inactive 2–3 hours; bake 35–45 minutes YIELD: 4–6 servings

Blueberry Brown Sugar Baked French Toast Topped with Toasted Pecans, Buttermilk Maple Syrup, and Whipped Cream

INGREDIENTS

4–5 cups chewy artisan bread, cubed

5 eggs

3 cups heavy cream

1 cup milk

1 cup dark brown sugar

2 teaspoons vanilla extract

1 teaspoon cinnamon

1 teaspoon kosher salt

1 cup frozen blueberries

3–4 tablespoons butter, cubed

TOPPINGS

2 cups Fresh Whipped Cream

1¼ cups Buttermilk Syrup

1 cup toasted pecans

½ cup butter

DIRECTIONS

Butter a 9-by-13-inch baking dish; set aside. Up to 2 days before serving, whisk the eggs, cream, milk, sugar, vanilla, cinnamon, and salt to form the custard base. Fold in the chewy bread. Pour the contents into the buttered casserole dish, cover with plastic wrap, and refrigerate for at least 2 to 3 hours (overnight is best).

To bake, preheat the oven to 350°. Remove the plastic wrap, sprinkle the blueberries on top, and dot with butter. Tuck and fold the blueberries into the bread gently so they don't crush. Allow the pan to sit on the counter for 10 minutes to take off the chill.

Bake for 35 to 45 minutes, until the casserole is puffed and golden. Top with the Buttermilk Syrup, toasted pecans, and some Fresh Whipped Cream.

CONTINUED

Blueberry Brown Sugar Baked French Toast Topped with Toasted Pecans, Buttermilk Maple Syrup, and Whipped Cream

FRESH WHIPPED CREAM

1½ cups heavy whipping cream
¼ cup sugar
1 pinch salt

BUTTERMILK SYRUP

1 cup good maple syrup
¼ cup full-fat buttermilk

FOR THE FRESH WHIPPED CREAM

Whisk all the ingredients, using a hand mixer or stand mixer, until soft peaks form.

FOR THE BUTTERMILK SYRUP

Simply mix the ingredients, and stir.

Great Falls, Montana.
Great-Gran Thora and
Great-Grandpa Danielson.

BREAKFAST 139

PREP TIME: 15 minutes COOK TIME: 12–18 minutes YIELD: 4 servings

Caramelized Onion Frittata

There might not be anything better than farm-fresh eggs. I mean the real deal: backyard chickens that eat apple skins and corn, run around your yard, and get picked up by the kids.

I can remember a day that was blustery and rainy; I was about eight years old. My mom and I were driving somewhere when we spotted a soft, white-and-tan chicken on the side of the road. She was soaking wet, her feathers droopy from all the rain. As my mom pulled over, she singlehandedly made all my dreams come true when she turned back to me and said, "Want to catch that chicken? We can take her home and have Dad build her a coop." We chased that chicken in the rain, up and down a white farm fence, and threw my oversize pink coat over her as a net. I held her on my lap the whole way home. I will never forget catching that little chicken. My dad built her a coop, and we bought several other chickens. We cared for them and loved that little brood.

Recently, when my own little family took a trip out to a dear friend's farm in Woodinville, Washington, to collect eggs, we chased down one of her pretty, fluffy, gray chickens so I could hold her. I immediately remembered being a kid and catching the tiny chicken that would become my friend when I was eight. At the Woodinville farm, Noah got to sprinkle corn and call the chickens in. I collected the most beautiful eggs. When we got home, I couldn't wait to clean them and make a gorgeous egg dish.

A frittata with caramelized onions, aged parmesan, gold potatoes, and thick-cut pepper bacon seemed like the responsible thing to do. After all, these were special eggs, in need of an extra-special recipe to make them shine! (You'll want to use a 12-inch, well-seasoned, cast-iron skillet.)

INGREDIENTS

1 large yellow onion, sliced thinly

5–6 slices thick-cut pepper bacon

1 tablespoon butter

2 medium Yukon Gold potatoes, diced

12 fresh eggs

½ cup milk or cream

1 cup grated parmesan cheese

Salt and pepper to taste

½ cup sliced green onions

DIRECTIONS

Preheat the oven to 350°. Sauté the onion and bacon in the butter over medium heat until the bacon is crispy and the onions are golden brown. Add the diced potatoes, and continue to cook for 7 to 8 minutes over medium heat.

In a separate bowl, crack all 12 eggs, mix with a whisk until the yolks are broken, and add the milk or cream, cheese, salt and pepper, and green onions. Mix completely. Pour the egg mixture over the hot bacon, onions, and potatoes. Immediately transfer to the oven, and bake for 12 to 18 minutes until the eggs are just set.

BREAKFAST 141

PREP TIME: 25 minutes COOK TIME: 10 minutes YIELD: 4 servings

Sweet Potato Hash and Fried Eggs

INGREDIENTS

2 sweet potatoes, diced into
 1-inch cubes

2 tablespoons olive oil, divided

Salt and pepper to taste

1 pound breakfast or country
 sausage

1 onion, diced

1 green bell pepper, chopped

3 cups baby spinach

1 pinch crushed red pepper
 flakes

6 eggs

DIRECTIONS

Preheat the oven to 350°. Line a baking sheet with parchment paper, and lay the potatoes on the parchment. Drizzle 1 tablespoon of oil on the potatoes, and season with salt and pepper. Bake for 25 minutes or until fork tender.

Meanwhile, heat a large skillet over medium heat, and brown the sausage in the remaining oil with the onion, pepper, and spinach. Season with the pepper flakes, salt, and pepper. Add the potatoes once they finish cooking, and sauté everything together for about 5 minutes. Crack the eggs into the hot skillet, and place it into the hot oven for 5 minutes.

Pull the skillet out, and let it stand for an additional 5 minutes before serving. Your eggs will have perfect, runny yolks. If you like the eggs cooked more, bake an additional 5 minutes.

Note: I definitely have a cheater method for a great hash: the potatoes seem to take so much longer to cook than everything else, so I roast them while everything else is frying in the skillet.

PREP TIME: 10 minutes COOK TIME: 15 minutes YIELD: 4–6 waffles

Whole-Grain Waffles with Apple Butterscotch Syrup

APPLE BUTTERSCOTCH SYRUP

1 apple, diced

1 teaspoon butter

1½ cups brown sugar

1 cup heavy cream

1 pinch salt

INGREDIENTS

1 cup whole-wheat flour

½ cup white all-purpose flour

2 cups whole milk

2 tablespoons baking powder

2 tablespoons brown sugar

2 tablespoons butter, melted

2 eggs

1 teaspoon salt

DIRECTIONS

Make the syrup first: Sauté the apple pieces in the butter, and add sugar, cream, and salt. Cook until the apples are soft and the sugar is completely dissolved into the cream, making a butterscotch.

To make the waffles, whisk together all the ingredients until they're just mixed; don't overmix. Butter the waffle iron, and fill it halfway; it'll spread to fill the iron perfectly. Serve with butter and a generous drizzle of the Apple Butterscotch Syrup.

PREP TIME: 10 minutes COOK TIME: 20 minutes
YIELD: 8–10 pancakes

Buttermilk Pumpkin Pancakes with Toasted Pecans and Cream Cheese Schmear

INGREDIENTS

1½ cups all-purpose flour

1 cup buttermilk

2 eggs

½ cup brown sugar

½ cup milk or cream

3 tablespoons pumpkin purée

2 tablespoons baking powder

2 tablespoons butter, melted

1 teaspoon vanilla extract

1 teaspoon cinnamon

1 dash salt

1–2 cups maple syrup

1 cup toasted pecans to
sprinkle on top

1 teaspoon butter per batch in
the pan

CREAM CHEESE SCHMEAR

8 ounces cream cheese

1 cup confectioners' sugar, plus
more for dusting

DIRECTIONS

Combine all the ingredients for the pancakes in a large bowl, and mix until just combined. Lumps are a good thing. Heat a nonstick skillet at medium heat for 5 minutes, then reduce the heat to low before you pour the first pancake. Use ⅓ to ½ cup for each pancake. Add 1 teaspoon butter to pan before frying each set of pancakes.

Cook on the first side of the pancake for 3 to 4 minutes, or until tiny bubbles appear on the surface of the pancakes, then flip! Cook an additional 2 minutes.

FOR THE CREAM CHEESE SCHMEAR

Warm the cream cheese for 30 seconds in the microwave, and stir in the confectioners' sugar. Mix until glossy and smooth. To serve, top the pancakes with a dollop of the warm cream cheese, a drizzle of syrup, and some toasted pecans.

FOR TOASTED PECANS

Toast the pecans in a 350° oven for 7 minutes on a cookie sheet.

PREP TIME: 10 minutes COOK TIME: 20–25 minutes YIELD: 4 servings

Fluffy Cornbread and Maple Syrup

Honey is just fine, but when I was little, we'd make cornbread for dinner, and any leftover pieces would get a nice pat of butter and a drizzle of maple syrup for warming up the next morning. Whipping the egg whites adds an extra lightness, and the butter in the batter makes it perfectly tender and salty.

INGREDIENTS

3 eggs, separated
1½ cups all-purpose flour
1½ cups cornmeal
1½ cups whole milk
1 cup sugar
½ cup butter, melted
1 tablespoon baking powder
1 tablespoon white vinegar
1 teaspoon salt
Butter for the skillet or pan and
  as topping
½ cup maple syrup, as topping

DIRECTIONS

Preheat the oven to 350°. Beat the egg whites to stiff peaks. Gently mix all the other ingredients, including the egg yolks, until they've just come together; fold in the egg whites, and pour into a generously buttered skillet. Bake for 20 to 25 minutes, or until a pick inserted in the center comes out clean.

If you are cooking in a cast-iron skillet, remove it from the oven when the cornbread is just barely done. The cast iron will continue to cook the cornbread, and you don't want it dry and crumbly.

Dot the warm cornbread with butter, and pour maple syrup over the top.

BREAKFAST 147

PREP TIME: 5 minutes COOK TIME: 5 minutes YIELD: 4 servings

Soft Scrambled Eggs

Slow and steady wins the race. Cooking eggs can be a very tricky business. I once read that in four-star restaurants in Paris, you are hired with a simple interview and cooking test: they see how well you can cook an egg. Seems simple, right? Well, it takes finesse and a level restraint to cook the perfect egg. These custard-like eggs are wonderful on buttered bread.

INGREDIENTS

2 tablespoons butter

6 eggs

½ cup heavy whipping cream

Salt and pepper to taste

½ cup shredded sharp cheddar cheese

¼ cup mild chèvre crumbles

4–6 slices crusty artisan bread, toasted

¼ cup chopped chives

DIRECTIONS

Heat a nonstick skillet to medium low, and add butter. Whisk together the eggs, cream, salt, and pepper; pour into the skillet. Gently fold the eggs over onto themselves, taking care to not break them up too much as they cook.

When these eggs are done, they are just cooked: only about 5 minutes; they'll be almost still glossy and creamy looking in some areas. Remove the pan from the heat, as the eggs will continue cooking.

Fold cheeses into the eggs, smear on toast, and sprinkle with chives.

PREP TIME: 5 minutes COOK TIME: 15 minutes YIELD: 6–8 pancakes

Chocolate Chip and Rye Pancakes

INGREDIENTS

1 cup all-purpose flour

1 cup buttermilk

1 cup chocolate chips

½ cup rye flour

½ cup brown sugar

½ cup milk or cream

2 eggs

2 tablespoons baking powder

2 tablespoons butter, melted

1 teaspoon vanilla extract

1 dash salt

DIRECTIONS

Combine all the ingredients in a large bowl, and mix until just combined. Lumps are a good thing. Heat a nonstick skillet at medium heat for 5 minutes, then reduce the heat to low before you pour the first pancake.

Add 1 teaspoon butter to pan before frying each set of pancakes. Cook on the first side of the pancake for 3 to 4 minutes, or until tiny bubbles appear on the surface of the pancakes, then flip! Cook an additional 2 minutes.

PREP TIME: 5 minutes COOK TIME: 5 minutes YIELD: 2 sandwiches

Bus-Stop Egg Sandwiches

I've never been a bowl-of-cereal girl to get my mornings going. My mom always indulged me in this growing up, and I loved her for it!

While the other kids in the family were having a bowl of fruity rings or Cheerios drowned in heaping tablespoons of sugar, I was having leftovers or microwaved round eggs on toasted English muffins.

Every morning, our house would be quiet, and all through junior high and high school, I'd be out the door at 6:00 a.m. with a microwaved egg sandwich in hand. We had a tool that cooked an egg in ninety seconds in the microwave. I loved that gadget. You cracked an egg into a round cup and put the lid on, and nine times out of ten, the egg would explode halfway through cooking but stay inside that cup. *Boom!* The egg explosion I expected—a hallmark sign the eggs were done. I didn't care. Massively overcooked eggs don't bother many fourteen-year-olds.

I would scrape the egg out of its terrible container and smash it into my buttered English muffin. Sometimes I'd throw a slice of cheese on the sandwich, but often it was just the egg and buttery bread. I'd normally have my sandwich eaten by the time I got to the bus stop.

One morning, I was running late, and I yelled to my older brother to make the bus driver wait. He protested, "No way, Danielle. C'mon!" I had to have my egg sandwich, but the microwave *was still cooking*. It finally finished after what seemed like hours, and I was flying out the door, backpack and coat in hand, running for the bus. I tucked my precious egg sandwich into the pocket of my coat.

Once I got to the bus, I thanked Mike, our bus driver, for waiting. I shuffled to the middle and took an empty row to myself. I took a moment to catch my breath and pulled my egg sandwich out and secretly tried to nibble at it so no one saw (no food allowed on the bus!). Moments later, a girl shrieked, "EWWWWW. What smells so bad?" Oh my gosh—it was my exploded radiation egg. I took a huge bite and hid my face, and she continued, "Mike! Someone's farting!" Ugh.

Her name was Stacie, and she was the bane of my existence (she nitpicked almost everything I did at the bus stop for three years until she moved). By this time, I could barely eat; I was embarrassed and worried about being found out. I shoveled the last bites of the sandwich into my mouth nervously. Stacie was only a row or two behind me. *Gulp*—it was finished. I turned around, only to catch eyes with Stacie, and she grunted, "Don't you smell it?"

BREAKFAST 151

CONTINUED

Bus-Stop Egg Sandwiches

I innocently said, "Smell what?" My heart was racing. Victory.

She rolled her eyes, and I'm sure she said something snarky back.

Eating that sandwich was easily the most stressful breakfast of my life, but she never found out. I continued to eat my sammies on the way to the bus stop and made sure they were gone before I got there.

This updated version of that classy egg sandwich has a tender egg, cooked in butter, with a jammy center and a crusty brown English muffin with herby butter. My egg sandwiches might have matured, but I'd never turn down a radiation-exploded egg if you offered it to me today.

Method is everything with a good fried egg. (I prefer my fried eggs cooked over low heat, in butter. You can keep all your crispy-edged fried eggs.)

INGREDIENTS

2 tablespoons butter

2 tablespoons your favorite tender herbs, like dill, tarragon, or flat-leaf parsley, chopped finely

2 eggs

2 English muffins

1 slice cheddar cheese (optional)

Flaky sea salt

DIRECTIONS

Gently smash butter and herbs together in a small bowl. Your herbed butter is done!

Melt a pat of butter in a small, nonstick frying pan over low heat, and crack eggs into the pan. Cook until the white is completely opaque. Flip, and cook about 30 to 40 more seconds. (I don't go for a runny yolk with this sandwich.)

Set the eggs aside, and toast the English muffins. Spread a generous amount of herbed butter and flaky salt on the bread. Place the slice of cheese over the butter and an egg on top. This might be one of the best sandwiches ever.

Yogurt Bowls with Stewed Apples

PREP TIME: 15 minutes YIELD: 4 servings

Yogurt Bowls with Stewed Apples

INGREDIENTS

2 cups whole milk, plain, or
Greek yogurt (see note)

2 cups your favorite granola

2 apples, cored and chopped

1 pear, chopped

½ cup brown sugar

1 tablespoon butter

1 pinch salt

⅓ cup toasted, sliced almonds
(optional)

DIRECTIONS

Simply place ½ cup yogurt in the bottom of a bowl, and top
with ½ cup granola.

Bring the apples, pear, sugar, butter, and salt to a simmer for
10 minutes. Spoon the stewed fruit over the cold yogurt and
granola. Sprinkle with the almonds, if desired.

*Note: This makes a lovely ice-cream bowl as well; use vanilla or custard
ice cream instead of yogurt.*

PREP TIME: 10 minutes COOK TIME: 25–30 minutes
YIELD: 4–6 servings

Baked Chiles Rellenos

INGREDIENTS

4–5 poblano peppers

8 eggs

3 tablespoons all-purpose flour

¾ cup heavy cream

Salt and pepper to taste

2 cups shredded sharp cheddar cheese

2 cups shredded Monterey Jack cheese

DIRECTIONS

Place the poblano peppers on a baking sheet, and turn the broiler to high. Broil each side of the pepper for 2 to 3 minutes, until the skins are blistered and black.

Remove peppers, put them in a paper bag, and allow them to sit for 5 to 7 minutes, until cool enough to handle. (The paper bag allows the skins to steam and separate from the flesh of pepper.) Remove skins and seeds.

Whisk the eggs, flour, cream, salt, and pepper together in a large bowl.

Butter a 9-by-13-inch glass baking dish, and add ⅓ of the egg mixture, ⅓ of the peppers, and ⅓ of the cheeses. Do this twice more, and finish with cheese. Refrigerate overnight.

To bake, preheat the oven to 350°, and remove casserole from the fridge at least 10 to 15 minutes before baking. Bake uncovered for 25 to 30 minutes, until eggs are set and the cheese is melted.

COOK TIME: 10 minutes YIELD: 4 servings

Cream of Wheat

I have learned so much in my short thirty-seven years. I've learned that failure is okay. I have learned that status means nothing. I have learned the greatest gift I will ever have or possess is my children and that they are in my safekeeping only until they are grown enough to forge their own way in this world. I have learned that my husband is my best companion, who has championed my dreams, no matter what they are. I have learned that simple is always best, and my heart will always lead me back to the Lord and my family, no matter where it's chosen to wander.

I am grateful for the gift of writing and communication, and even if it's the simplest recipe in this book, it's nourishing and filled with memories. This one reminds me of winter. Winters in life are just seasons; spring will always come. The thaw will happen, and life has its fiery times, but fires lead to great change and rebirth. This is more of a memory than a recipe. This is true, simple comfort food.

The box says to mix the dry cereal with water, but I always make it with milk.

INGREDIENTS

3 cups whole milk

1 pinch salt

½ cup Cream of Wheat cereal

2 tablespoons butter

½ cup brown sugar

DIRECTIONS

Bring the milk and salt to a simmer, and add the dry cereal. Once it's creamy and finished, about 5 to 7 minutes, add the butter and brown sugar on top. Don't mix it; just let it melt. Blueberries are wonderful on this.

BREAKFAST 157

Drinks

A Talk with Gloria

When I was writing this book, I called my grandmother Gloria to talk about life. We discussed how she grew up and also how her mama grew up. When my grandmother calls her mother, Thora, "Mama," it sounds like music as she, ever so lovingly, almost *sings* the word. Her eyes draw down and the corners of her mouth draw up in sad delight. She loved her mama very much; Mama was her friend and confidante.

Everyone who knew Thora loved her. She had a big, bright, sassy smile, and what she said went. To think that her career in cooking somehow gave way to mine is a treasured notion. While my grandmother and I talked, we laughed as she remembered small details about her school days. Then, reaching further back in time, she told me how Thora grew up on a dairy farm. We discussed the stuff of life: triumphs and struggles, stories and lessons.

It's important to remember where we come from in order to know where we are going. I will treasure every talk with my grandmother along with every memory passed down. These memories have been and always will be the foundation on which I build my life and my children's lives. We will one day sit down with a cup of coffee to talk about the past and hope for the future.

There is comfort in a drink. For children, it's there in a cup of milk. As we age, it's there in wine and champagne for celebration or root beer floats to share with our babies. It's there when we raise toasts to the bright days to come. When even more years pass, we'll sit down with that same cup of comfort to warm our bones on cold days and sip to happy times gone by. Drinks are more than just an accompaniment; they are a salve for tough times as well as a necessary component when building a meal.

PREP TIME: 10 minutes YIELD: 1½ to 2 quarts

Old-Fashioned Lemonade

INGREDIENTS

1 cup freshly squeezed lemon juice (4–5 lemons)

1½ cups sugar

2–4 cups water

DIRECTIONS

Squeeze the lemons, and add the juice to the sugar. Stir to completely incorporate. Allow to sit for about 10 minutes or until the sugar granules have completely dissolved. Add the water, starting with 2 cups, then adding an additional cup to suit your own lemonade tastes.

PREP TIME: 5 minutes YIELD: 4–6 servings

Grapefruit Paloma

INGREDIENTS

2 cups freshly squeezed grapefruit juice

3 ounces vodka, tequila, or raki

1 cup ice

1 bunch mint, chopped, about ½ cup

3 tablespoons lemon simple syrup (see note)

2 tablespoons lime juice

Mint to garnish

DIRECTIONS

I make this drink in two batches: place half the ingredients in a cocktail shaker, shake vigorously, and strain into chilled martini glasses or pour over ice. Repeat.

Note: To make the simple syrup, boil 1 cup water with the zest of 1 lime or lemon and 1 cup sugar. Cool. Syrup lasts in the fridge for up to 10 days.

DRINKS

PREP TIME: 5 minutes COOK TIME: 5–7 minutes YIELD: 4–6 servings

Hot Chocolate

INGREDIENTS

6 cups whole milk (see note)

1 cup brown sugar

1 cup unsweetened cocoa
powder

2 teaspoons vanilla extract

1 shy teaspoon kosher salt

Whipped cream and chocolate
shavings for garnish (optional)

DIRECTIONS

Bring the first 5 ingredients to a simmer over medium heat.
Whisk for 5 minutes, until the sugar has dissolved and the
cocoa has absorbed into the milk. Serve with whipped cream
and chocolate shavings.

*Note: Hot milk loves to boil over. Take care to not overheat the milk, and
if it begins to boil, promptly remove it from the heat.*

PREP TIME: 5 minutes YIELD: 4–6 servings

Cider Champagne Cocktail

INGREDIENTS

1 (750 mL) bottle champagne
or prosecco

2½ cups fresh-pressed apple
cider

2 cinnamon sticks

1 thinly sliced apple

DIRECTIONS

For every bottle of your fave champagne or prosecco, combine
with 2½ cups fresh-pressed apple cider, 2 cinnamon sticks, and
1 thinly sliced apple.

PREP TIME: 5 minutes YIELD: 1 (8-ounce) serving

Italian Sodas

It's 1992, and you are in third grade. You got a B on your spelling exam, and you are not particularly good at spelling, so you celebrate the victory with blackberry Italian sodas! The anticipation, the sweet swirl of victory as the coffee stand barista (just called "worker" back then) sets the sixteen-ounce clear plastic cup on the counter. She places simple syrup in the bottom of the cup, tops it with ice, adds club soda, and then the miracle happens: she slowly pours the cream into the cup, and the crowd goes wild! I (the crowd) sit and ponder our next treat for a great day at school and love Mom even more for thinking of it.

Okay, so maybe you are not a third-grade spelling struggler sipping sweet victory after your win, but you love these sodas. No matter who you are, the words *Italian soda* will walk you immediately down memory lane: syrups, seltzer waters, and cream—every kid's dream. For adults, maybe insert a shot of booze just before that famous cream float to finish it off.

What is an Italian soda? How does one achieve hero status involving simple syrups made from fruit and bliss? The Italian soda was invented in 1925 in the North Beach neighborhood of San Francisco by Italian American immigrants. Originally, they didn't have any cream finish, just sweet syrup and seltzer. However, the ones I grew up on always had cream in them, and these are actually called cremosas or French sodas.

There are three major components to an Italian soda: the syrup, ice, and seltzer. That's it. But if you're into happiness, the fourth must is cream.

Generally speaking, you need one part syrup and one part ice to one part seltzer or club soda, and one part cream to finish: four parts total. If you want these loaded, add the liquor to the syrup base and proceed.

A few weeks back, my oldest son asked for a glass of juice while we were out. He really wanted some juice. Being the awesome mom that I am, I thought, *Hey, I've got one lemon. I can make you a glass of lemonade!* I squeezed the lemon in the bottom of the glass, added two tablespoons of honey, and just as I was about to add the water, I thought, *WAIT! Let me cover this with ice, pour seltzer on top, and float the cream!* Soon, we were enjoying this wonderful lemony, honey, creamy treat, and I was again a superhero to my boy. Have fun with this—the sky is really the limit.

164 DRINKS

CONTINUED

Italian Sodas

INGREDIENTS (OPTIONS)

Real fruit smashed with sugar or agave to make a sweet fruity base.

Any simple syrup. Chocolate syrup. Herb-infused syrups.

Chai! Get out that amazing carton of chai, and turn it into an Italian soda.

Kitschy canned nectars. You know what I'm talking about—guava and mango, borderline too-thick-to-drink but begging to be mixed up in an Italian soda.

What about the syrups you had as a kid? Dump a few melted frozen treats like Otter Pops in your glass.

THE SELTZER (OPTIONS)

Seltzer

Club soda

Sprite

Think clear and fizzy. Heck, even champagne might be fun. Slowly pour your clear, fizzy seltzer of choice over the ice, leaving enough room at the top for that splash of cream.

THE GLASS

Technically, you can use any type of glass, but an Italian soda really lends itself to a tall, clear glass. Italian sodas are as much about the process as they are about the ingredients. You really want to see what's going on.

THE SYRUP

Choose your syrup, then place a fair amount in the bottom of your glass. The syrup can be any number of things (see options in the Ingredients list to the left).

THE ICE

You might not think ice is significant, but the ice structure actually aids in the swirling and acts as a buffer between the seltzer and the syrup. So choose any ice: cubed, crushed, flaked. *But don't skip the ice!* Pick your favorite ice, and fill the glass ½ to ¾ full.

THE METHOD

The method is simple: heavy syrup on the bottom of the glass, cover with ice, slowly pour your choice of seltzer over the top (see options in the Seltzer list to the left), and then gently float the cream. That's it!

THE CREAM

If you are a purist, skip this step, but if you are a decent human, add that cream. Slowly pour the cream into the glass until you see the swirls start to happen, then *stop*.

PREP TIME: 5–7 minutes YIELD: 4–6 (8-ounce) cups

Egg Coffee

I called my grandmother Gloria several years ago when I first conceptualized this book. I asked her about how she grew up, and I wanted to hear from her mouth what she loved about her mother. She told me she would give anything in the world to have just another slice of her mother's lemon chiffon pie, and she told me how her mama made egg coffee. It's very Norwegian (Uff-da!). It's such a curious way to make coffee, and it yields a rich, full-bodied elixir that warms the soul and smells like heaven. The aroma fills the home because it's boiled on the stove for three to five minutes. You can make this in a large pot or a percolator without the top pieces. Pour it through a strainer if you like it smoother, but this method helps sink the grounds with the help of that egg. To see my grandma smile with such a glimmer when she talks about her mother is a lovely thing. She celebrates her eighty-third birthday this year, and I am going to serve her a slice of lemon chiffon pie and a cup of egg coffee. My pie won't be as perfect as Great-Gran Thora's, but I'll give it a shot.

INGREDIENTS

6 tablespoons coffee, medium grind

1 egg, shell and all

DIRECTIONS

Smash the egg into a small bowl with the shell, add the coffee, and make a slurry. Bring 7 cups of water to a boil, and quickly whisk in the egg-and-coffee mixture. Stir, and let steep/simmer for 3 to 5 minutes. When the coffee has brewed, pour ½ cup ice-cold water into the pot or percolator. The cool water helps the grounds and egg sink to the bottom of the pot. The eggshells take away some of the bitter taste in the coffee and create a smoother cup of joe.

PREP TIME: 5 minutes YIELD: 4 servings

Mojito Floats

INGREDIENTS

24 ounces limeade

4 ounces dark rum

¾ cup finely chopped fresh
mint

1 pint Snoqualmie Ice Cream
Lime Sorbet

DIRECTIONS

Place the mint, dark rum, and limeade in the blender. Pulse to chop the mint. Place 2 scoops of lime sorbet in a 12-ounce tumbler, and top with the blended juice. Garnish with mint, and enjoy!

Sweets

One of the defining desserts of my childhood was a slice of yellow cake with a dark and soft fudge frosting. The cake was a box mix, and the frosting came from a plastic tub. I think it cost all of a buck and a quarter for the mix and the frosting. One 9-by-13-inch aluminum pan made twelve slices. Everyone in my house got two pieces. I'd let the other kids get their slices first because I wanted the center slices. In the cake's center, the frosting was thicker and the cake was never dry. I'd eat one slice, then save the other for breakfast. It was a rewarding and delicious bit of strategy.

I learned at a young age that life is worth celebrating, no matter what. Sometimes we'd make cake because the day was tough, and many times we'd make cake because *any* day is a good day for a cake. Sweets can bring such joy. They represent—more than any other part of a meal—pure nostalgia. One bite, and all of a sudden, like a magic trick, you are transported to the place in time when you first indulged. Perhaps it's in your childhood home or your grandmother's kitchen. Maybe you are in the cafeteria line at school during a time when school lunch was homemade and from scratch, prepared by a bunch of mothers making gravies like their mamas did and baking off apple pies to load onto the lunch trays. We all have places in our past to which the right sweet confection helps us to return.

My mother's favorite desserts are a slice of pie alongside white cake with buttercream frosting because when she was a little girl, the lunch lady at her elementary school gave her a small slice of each even though the rules said she was supposed to choose just one. That kindness stuck with her.

To this day, nothing takes me back like a slice of buttery yellow cake with chocolate frosting.

PREP TIME: 10 minutes COOK TIME: 25–30 minutes
YIELD: 1 9×13-inch cake or 2 8-inch round cakes

Aunt Libby's Carrot Cake

INGREDIENTS

4 eggs

$2/3$ cup grapeseed oil

½ cup butter, melted

¼ cup cream

1 teaspoon vanilla extract

2¼ cups all-purpose flour

1½ cups brown sugar

2 teaspoons baking powder

1 teaspoon baking soda

1 teaspoon cinnamon

½ teaspoon salt

4 cups grated carrots

1 cup chopped walnuts

1 cup chopped golden raisins

FROSTING

8 ounces cream cheese,
   softened

½ cup butter, softened

Splash of vanilla extract

2½–3 cups confectioners' sugar

1 pinch salt

Splash of milk or cream
   (optional)

DIRECTIONS

Preheat the oven to 350°. Mix the wet ingredients; fold in the dry up to the salt, and stir until it's almost mixed; add carrots, nuts, and raisins, and mix until it just comes together.

Bake in a buttered and floured 9-by-13-inch pan for 25 to 30 minutes or until a pick comes out clean.

FOR THE FROSTING

Add enough confectioners' sugar to the cream cheese, butter, vanilla, and salt to make it how ya like it—maybe 2½ or 3 cups—and mix. Add a splash of milk or cream to thin if needed.

SWEETS 173

PREP TIME: 10 minutes **COOK TIME:** 30–35 minutes
YIELD: 1 9×13-inch cake or 2 8-inch round cakes

Cherry Chip Cake with Cream Cheese Icing

INGREDIENTS

½ cup butter, softened

1½ cups sugar

1 teaspoon vanilla extract

1 teaspoon almond extract

1 teaspoon kosher salt

4 egg whites

2 tablespoons mild oil, suitable for baking

½ cup heavy whipping cream

2¼ cups all-purpose flour, spooned and leveled

1 tablespoon baking powder

½ cup finely diced maraschino cherries

CREAM CHEESE ICING

4 cups confectioners' sugar

8 ounces cream cheese, softened

½ cup butter, softened

1 pinch salt

Splash of almond extract

DIRECTIONS

Preheat the oven to 350°. Cream the butter, sugar, vanilla extract, almond extract, and salt until light and fluffy, making sure to scrape down the sides of the bowl. Add the egg whites one at a time, beating after each addition. Add oil, and beat until the batter becomes smooth. Scrape down the sides of the bowl. Slowly add whipping cream as the mixer is running.

While this beats for 3 minutes, whisk flour and baking powder in a separate bowl. Fold flour into the batter in three parts. Gently fold cherries into the batter. Mix only until it's just incorporated.

Pour into two 8-inch cake pans or a 9-by-13-inch baking dish. Bake for 30 to 35 minutes or until a pick comes out clean.

FOR THE CREAM CHEESE ICING

Cream all the ingredients until smooth.

PREP TIME: 10 minutes **COOK TIME:** 25–35 minutes
YIELD: 1 9×13-inch cake or 2 8-inch round cakes

Chocolate Buttermilk Birthday Cake with Malted Chocolate Cream Cheese Frosting

INGREDIENTS

1¾ cups all-purpose flour

1½ cups sugar

1 cup full-fat buttermilk

½ cup unsweetened cocoa
  powder

½ cup vegetable oil

2 eggs

1 tablespoon instant coffee

1 tablespoon vanilla extract

2 teaspoons baking powder

1 teaspoon kosher salt

½ teaspoon baking soda

¾ cup boiling water

MALTED CREAM CHEESE FROSTING

3 cups confectioners' sugar

8 ounces cream cheese,
  softened

½ cup butter, softened

2 tablespoons cocoa powder

2 tablespoons vanilla malt
  powder

Milk to thin, if needed

FOR THE CAKE

Preheat the oven to 350°. Butter and flour two round 8-inch
cake pans. Mix all the ingredients except the boiling water in
the bowl of a stand mixer until smooth. Add boiling water and
mix for 15–20 seconds.

Pour the thin batter into buttered and floured cake pans (we
sometimes do a 9-by-13 one as well). Bake for 30 minutes or
until a pick comes out clean. Do not overbake.

FOR THE FROSTING

Mix until it's your desired consistency, and spread on the
cooled cake.

SWEETS 175

PREP TIME: 10 minutes COOK TIME: 35–40 minutes
YIELD: 1 standard 9×3-inch Bundt pan

Grandma Hawkins's Applesauce Bundt Cake

INGREDIENTS

2 cups applesauce

1 teaspoon baking soda

1 cup brown sugar

¾ cup granulated sugar

½ cup butter

1 tablespoon olive oil

2 teaspoons vanilla extract

2 teaspoons kosher salt

2 eggs

2 cups all-purpose flour

1 teaspoon apple pie spice or cinnamon

DIRECTIONS

Preheat the oven to 350°. Add the baking soda to the applesauce and set aside. Cream the sugars with the butter, oil, vanilla, and salt. Add the eggs, then mix until it just comes together. Combine the flour and spice in a separate bowl. Gently fold the applesauce mixture and the flour into the sugar mixture, alternating between them, in three separate additions. Do not overmix.

Generously butter and flour a Bundt pan, and spoon the batter into the pan. Bake for 40 minutes or until a pick comes out clean.

Dust with confectioners' sugar.

Note: Allow the baked cake to cool for exactly 15 minutes, then whack the pan a few times firmly all over. Place a plate or cooling rack on top of the cake pan, then quickly invert it onto the plate. It should come out perfectly every time.

Southern California. Great-Grandma Hawkins and my dad, Michael.

176 SWEETS

PREP TIME: 10 minutes COOK TIME: 15–18 minutes
YIELD: 1 9×13-inch pan

Cream Cheese Brownies

BROWNIE MIXTURE

4 eggs

2 cups sugar

1 cup butter, melted

½ teaspoon salt

1 teaspoon vanilla extract

¾ cup cocoa powder (Dutch process recommended)

1 shy cup flour

1 teaspoon baking powder

1 cup bittersweet chocolate chips

CREAM CHEESE FILLING

8 ounces cream cheese, room temperature

1 egg yolk

½ cup sugar

DIRECTIONS

Preheat the oven to 350°. Line a 9-by-13-inch pan with parchment paper; set aside. Combine all the ingredients for the brownie mixture in order in a large mixing bowl, and mix until they are just mixed together. Spoon or pour the batter into the parchment-lined pan.

Mix the filling ingredients in a separate mixing bowl until smooth with no lumps, then spoon it into 12 even dollops all over your brownie mix in the pan.

Drag a butter knife through each dollop of cream cheese to make swirls. When your swirls are to your liking, place the pan in the oven for 15 minutes. Rotate the pan, and bake for 3 to 5 more minutes.

These brownies cook quickly. Carefully watch toward the end to make sure they don't overbake. There should be a slight amount of give in the center when fully baked.

COOK TIME: 10 minutes YIELD: 2 cups

Spiced Stewed Apples

INGREDIENTS

2 apples, chopped
1 pear, chopped
½ cup brown sugar
1 tablespoon butter
½ teaspoon pumpkin pie spice
1 pinch salt

DIRECTIONS

Bring everything to a simmer; cook only about 10 minutes so the fruit retains its shape. The pear will give way for a lovely sauce. Fresh woodsy herbs like rosemary or thyme are great in this if you are adventurous. Remove the herbs before serving.

Great Falls, Montana.
Great-Grandpa Danielson and
baby Great-Uncle Dick.

SWEETS

PREP TIME: 20–25 minutes COOK TIME: 15 minutes YIELD: 12 pies

Dark Chocolate and Cherry Cream Cheese Whoopie Pies

CAKE

½ cup butter, softened

1 cup sugar

2 eggs

1 teaspoon vanilla extract

2 cups all-purpose flour

¼ cup unsweetened cocoa powder

1 teaspoon salt

1 teaspoon baking soda

1 teaspoon baking powder

1 cup cream

FILLING

4 tablespoons butter, softened

1 (8-ounce) package cream cheese, softened

1 (13-ounce) container marshmallow cream

½ cup confectioners' sugar

1 cup diced fancy dessert cherries

DIRECTIONS

Preheat the oven to 350°. Line a baking sheet with parchment. Cream together the butter and sugar until fluffy, then add eggs one at a time, beating until each is just incorporated.

Add the vanilla and dry ingredients. Mix for 15 to 20 seconds, then add half of the cream, mix an additional 15 to 20 seconds, and add the rest of the cream. Mix batter until it's just come together.

Use a self-releasing ice-cream scoop to scoop 12 cookies onto the baking sheet. Bake for 12 to 15 minutes, and repeat. Cool completely before filling.

FOR THE FILLING

Place the butter and cream cheese into the bowl of a stand mixer, or use a hand mixer to mix slowly until completely smooth. Add the marshmallow cream, then the confectioners' sugar. Mix. (I added just 1 drop of all-natural red food coloring for a pale-pink filling.)

Next, fold the chopped cherries in by hand. Add a hefty dollop of filling to 12 of the cookies, then top with another cookie to make a pie!

SWEETS 181

PREP TIME: 10 minutes COOK TIME: 30–40 minutes
YIELD: 1 standard 9×3-inch Bundt pan

Coconut Bundt Cake with Lemon Curd, Toasted Coconut, and Soft Whipped Cream

Super-moist and dreamy, this foolproof cake will make your mama proud! Mother's Day is really all about spoiling the moms in our lives. Nowadays, my family eats a delicious brunch, complete with champagne, and finishes with a light and lemony dessert. The average lemon dessert gets a coconutty makeover this year that's going to make fans out of your entire family.

CAKE

2 cups all-purpose flour

1½ cups sugar

½ cup coconut cream (from a can)

½ cup heavy cream

½ cup oil suitable for baking

3 eggs

1 teaspoon coconut extract

1 teaspoon vanilla extract

½ cup boiling water

TOPPINGS

1 cup lemon curd

2 cups fresh, soft whipped cream

1 cup toasted coconut flakes

DIRECTIONS

Preheat the oven to 350°. Mix all cake ingredients except the boiling water in the bowl of a stand mixer until smooth. Turn the mixer to low, slowly stream the boiling water into the batter, and mix for 45 seconds.

Pour batter into a buttered and floured Bundt pan. Bake for 40 minutes or until the top is lightly golden brown and a pick inserted comes out almost clean; the cake will continue to bake once it's pulled from the oven.

Cool cake for 10 minutes, then run a knife along all the outer and inner edges to loosen it from the Bundt pan. Place a plate on top, and while holding each side firmly, quickly flip the cake over. The cake should release with no problem.

Allow to cool completely before adding toppings. Then spoon the lemon curd, whipped cream, and toasted coconut over the top of the cake.

182 SWEETS

PREP TIME: 10 minutes COOK TIME: 45 minutes
YIELD: 1 9×13-inch pan

Coconut Cream Lemon Bars

CRUST

2 cups all-purpose flour

1 cup butter, softened

½ cup sugar

½ teaspoon kosher salt

FILLING

1 (14.5-ounce) can cream of
coconut, such as Coco Lopez

2 cups sugar

5 large eggs

1 cup fresh lemon or lime juice
(I use half a cup of each)

Zest of 2 lemons (about 2
heaping tablespoons)

½ cup all-purpose flour

½ teaspoon kosher salt

½ teaspoon pure coconut
extract

1 cup sweetened shredded
coconut

DIRECTIONS

Preheat the oven to 350°. Mix the ingredients for the crust in
the bowl of a stand mixer or by hand until they come together.
It may be a bit crumbly, and that's okay.

Press into the bottom of a 9-by-13-inch baking dish, and bake
for about 15 minutes, until the top has just begun to show signs
of browning.

FOR THE FILLING

Add the coconut cream to a mixing bowl along with the sugar.
Mix with a whisk. Slowly add each egg so you get a smooth,
creamy-textured filling with no lumps.

Add the lemon juice, lemon zest, flour, salt, and extract.
Mix, and pour over baked and slightly cooled crust. Add the
shredded coconut to the top.

Bake for 25 to 30 minutes, or until the center has just set and
no longer wobbles but has not cracked.

SWEETS 185

Honey Butter Biscuit Strawberry Shortcake

PREP TIME: 45 minutes YIELD: 8–10 biscuits

Honey Butter Biscuit Strawberry Shortcake

During my time at Minoela, my old bistro, we served fresh, homemade, buttery pound cakes with brown sugar cream and fresh berries. It was by far one of the most popular items on our sweets menu. In the summer months, I could barely keep pound cake and cream in stock. For almost three years, from the day we opened, a man came in from across the street once a week. It was his favorite. I began to see less and less of him and learned he had become ill. He'd call in an order, and a friend would come get it for him. One evening, he came in a wheelchair and was on oxygen; he and his family ate that cake and laughed and cried. I hid in the kitchen and cried a little too. My place had become his place. The following week, his family came in, but he wasn't there. They had two orders of his favorite shortcakes, and they talked and laughed and cried. How special this life is. I had no idea at the time, but what I was doing wasn't really about food at all. The coming years would prove this in the sweetest way.

Five years ago, roughly to the day our restaurant closed its doors, Michael packed our car with the remaining supplies after our massive sidewalk sale, and we had to take home loads of pound cakes and gallons of heavy whipping cream. I was at home with a tiny, fresh, beautiful baby, and in the weeks to come, this would prove to be the most wonderful time in my life. Mike was tying up all the loose ends, and when he got home, I wrapped and froze the cakes and cream.

We had no money. We had no business. I do remember feeling a sense of relief in the turmoil: now we pick up the pieces. I stopped cooking. Our marriage was in a rocky place, but now, all of the sudden, we were a family. We were home together; we were in love with our son. I had never in my life experienced love like that: so deep I'd cry because I felt so lucky to finally have this sweet baby boy.

For dinner in those days, we had pound cake and soft whipped cream and fruit. I remember sitting on our bed and talking again, like we used to: about life, our family, what we hoped would be next. We did this nightly until the cake and cream ran out. We fell in love again over strawberry shortcakes and a sleeping baby.

I had long forgotten this sweet memory until last week at my dear friend Malia's house; we were talking and laughing, and she set out everything for shortcakes. She whipped cream, and we chatted about life and the plans God had, about our families and futures. My time with her is precious. We can be ourselves with no pressure. She plated my shortcake and doused it in

CONTINUED

Honey Butter Biscuit Strawberry Shortcake

cream and berries, and I felt immensely loved. As I drove home from our visit, I remembered when Mike and I began to heal over buttery cake, whipped cream, and berries. Even in the darkest times, there is hope, life, and beauty. I have been thinking of pound cakes, shortcakes, proper cream, and berries daily ever since.

Yesterday morning, I had a wonderful visit with a dear new friend, Sarah; she invited us to her home to pick fresh figs. These aren't just any figs; they are big, beautiful Desert King figs—or pigs, as her sweet daughter calls them. The outer skin is a bright, vivid green, and the interior flesh is the deepest rose pink. I shared my story about how our life got very hard and then God loved me enough to strip everything away and heal my marriage through a new beginning and a family I had only hoped for. It reminded me that I need to keep sharing, keep telling people the goodness of our heavenly Father in broken times, in my brokenness. We left feeling refreshed, and I headed to my mom's house. When the evening came, I broke out everything to make berry shortcakes. Noah called back to my dad, "Papa, we made you sweets for dinner!" As I split open the cake and poured the cream over the top and put diced, fresh figs and berries on top of that, I was completely in awe of what my life looks like now: so richly blessed with friendship and family, a healthy marriage to a man I was once too selfish to see had a heart of gold, and no more bucket list. Everything I ever dreamed of doing, I've done. I broke off a hunk of cake, dunked it into the sweet, soft whipped cream, and thanked God for my life. It isn't perfect—I have so much room to grow, and I've never been happier.

When I think back to my days at Minoela, I thought I was on top of the world, but I was… alone. Unhappy, chasing a financial dream through food. When people ask me now what I do for a living, I sometimes stumble through my words, trying to articulate everything, all the jobs I have and everything I do, but as of late, we have truly solidified that Rustic Joyful Food isn't really in the food business at all; we are in the people business, and I happen to be using food to do it. My love for people and nurturing people's hearts far surpasses my love of cooking or business or styling.

You might have a story that someone needs to hear to feel encouraged and to feel like there is hope in a dark time. Never stop sharing. Never stop dreaming or believing you have a purpose that shines so brightly and can't be diminished by anyone or anything. Please, eat all the shortcakes.

CONTINUED

Honey Butter Biscuit Strawberry Shortcake

INGREDIENTS

½ cup cold butter, diced into cubes and smooshed into flat disks

2¼ cups all-purpose flour, plus more for dusting

1 teaspoon salt

2 tablespoons baking powder

1 cup heavy whipping cream

2 tablespoons honey

FRESH STRAWBERRIES

3–4 cups fresh strawberries

½ cup brown sugar

2 tablespoons fresh lemon juice

1 pinch salt

CRÈME FRAÎCHE WHIPPED CREAM

1 cup crème fraîche

1 cup heavy whipping cream

½ cup confectioners' sugar

1 teaspoon vanilla extract

1 pinch salt

FOR THE BISCUITS

Preheat the oven to 400°. Pulse the butter, flour, salt, and baking powder in the bowl of a food processor. Whisk the cream and honey in another bowl. Slowly add the honeyed cream to the flour mixture, and pulse a few times until the mix comes together to form a shaggy dough. Dump the contents onto a floured surface, and form into a 10-by-6-inch rectangle. Fold the rectangle in half, and place in the fridge to rest for at least 30 minutes.

When dough has rested, roll out into another 10-by-6 rectangle, and fold over on itself. Roll a 10-by-6 rectangle a third and final time. Use a serrated bread knife to slice the dough into 9 pieces without pressing it down too hard. Press the biscuits into a buttered muffin tin or arrange on a baking sheet.

Brush the tops of the biscuits with melted butter and a drizzle of honey before baking. Bake for about 15 minutes, until puffed and golden.

FOR THE BERRIES

Simply wash and slice the berries in half, then gently fold into the sugar, lemon juice, and salt. Allow to stand at room temp for at least 30 minutes so the berries can make a nice syrup with their own juices.

FOR THE CREAM

Combine all the ingredients, then whip on high, just until soft peaks form.

PREP TIME: 5 minutes COOK TIME: 1 minute YIELD: 1 serving

Mug Cakes, a.k.a. the Emotional Support Treat

It's late, it's been a heck of a day, you're tired, your sweet tooth is *on*, and you are rummaging through the cupboards, about to eat a spoonful of peanut butter and some old raisins just to keep the beast at bay. Then, suddenly, out of nowhere, you remember last night, aimlessly scrolling through Pinterest, imagining that you're the genius party planner, the artsy mom who fabricates crazy-cool hair bows on the side, the industrious thrift-store scavenger reupholstering mid-mod dining chairs. And what's this, Pinterest? What's this delectable delight? The *mug cake*! Forty-five seconds to molten bliss. You are skeptical but desperate, so you give it a go. Flour—check! You've got a bag of flour. Sugar—sure, everyone's got sugar. No eggs...grrr. Wait! No problem; Pinterest said this is better. Butter? Well, duh, you've got butter AND that peanut butter...standby. Cocoa powder—do we have this? Aunt Edna brought cocoa powder last Christmas for real hot cocoa. You find it and get to mixing in your mug. Mind explosion! The day's woes slip away like a silk sheet. You say, "Self, am I really having a brownie-like cake right now? Three minutes ago, I was about to lick the sides of the empty maple syrup container, and now *I'm saved*...by what is basically an Easy-Bake Oven treat for grown-ups. Nice job, self."

INGREDIENTS

3 tablespoons all-purpose flour

2 tablespoons brown sugar

1 tablespoon cocoa powder

¼ teaspoon baking powder

2 tablespoons butter, softened

1 tablespoon milk

1 tablespoon liquid mix-in
   (peanut butter, hot fudge,
   Nutella, etc.)

1 pinch salt

DIRECTIONS

Pick a heatproof 12-ounce mug. Mix the dry ingredients in the mug, then add all the wet ingredients. Mix. It might seem like there isn't enough moisture—don't add more; just keep mixing. Mix until thick. Push batter into bottom of the mug. Microwave for 45 seconds, no more than 1 minute.

Add mix-ins to your heart's content: nuts, candy, chocolate chips, etc. Enjoy.

PREP TIME: 5 minutes COOK TIME: 35–45 minutes
YIELD: 1 standard 9×5×2.5-inch loaf pan

Molasses and Walnut Zucchini Bread

INGREDIENTS

2 cups grated zucchini

1½ cups packed dark brown
   sugar

2 eggs

⅓ cup olive oil

⅛ cup molasses

2 teaspoons vanilla extract

1 teaspoon cinnamon

1 teaspoon kosher salt

2 cups all-purpose flour

2 teaspoons baking powder

½ teaspoon baking soda

1 cup chopped walnuts

DIRECTIONS

Preheat the oven to 350°. Line a loaf pan with parchment paper. Mix the zucchini, sugar, eggs, oil, molasses, vanilla, cinnamon, and salt until well combined.

Fold in the flour, baking powder, and baking soda. Mix until it just comes together, then fold in the walnuts. Do not overmix.

Pour the batter into the loaf pan, and bake for 35 to 45 minutes or until a pick inserted in the center of the loaf comes out clean.

PREP TIME: 5 minutes COOK TIME: 25–30 minutes
YIELD: 1 9×13-inch pan

Pineapple and Cherry Crumble

This is a simple homage to the dump cakes of my childhood.

INGREDIENTS

2 cups chopped pineapple,
  canned or fresh

1 (24-ounce) can pie cherries

CRUMBLE

1¾ cups all-purpose flour

1 cup butter

¾ cup sugar

1 teaspoon kosher salt

DIRECTIONS

Mix the crumble ingredients in the bowl of a stand mixer or
with a hand mixer until soft and crumbly.

Preheat the oven to 350°. Spoon the pineapple into the bottom
of a buttered 9-by-13-inch pan. Evenly spread the cherries over
the top, then do the same with the crumble.

Bake for 25 to 30 minutes until the fruit is bubbling and the
crumble is a light golden brown.

PREP TIME: 5 minutes YIELD: 3 cups

Cream Cheese and Honey Fruit Dip

INGREDIENTS

8 ounces cream cheese,
  softened

¼ cup honey

½ teaspoon kosher salt

2 cups heavy whipping cream

3–4 cups sliced fresh fruit, like
  strawberries, apple slices,
  pineapple chunks, or pears

DIRECTIONS

Whip the cream cheese with the honey and salt in the bowl of
a stand mixer or with a hand mixer, then slowly pour in the
cream. Whip until it's fluffy and thickened. Serve with fresh
fruit. This keeps up to 3 days in the refrigerator.

PREP TIME: 5 minutes COOK TIME: 35–45 minutes
YIELD: 1 9-inch deep-dish pie

Walnut Pie

INGREDIENTS

3 eggs

2 cups dark brown sugar

2 cups chopped walnuts

½ cup butter, melted

2 tablespoons bourbon or
  whiskey

2 teaspoons vanilla extract

1 teaspoon kosher salt

SHORTBREAD CRUST

2 cups all-purpose flour

1 cup butter, softened

¼ cup sugar

1 teaspoon salt

DIRECTIONS

Preheat the oven to 350°. Mix the crust, and press ¾ of it in the bottom of a deep-dish pie plate.

Mix all filling ingredients and pour directly into the crust. Sprinkle remaining ¼ of the crust mixture on top of the walnut center. Bake for 35 to 45 minutes.

Nut pies should always have a tiny wiggle in the middle; if it's not moving when nudged, it's overbaked. The pie will continue to set outside the oven. Cool for 4 hours before serving, but it won't hurt a thing to try it sooner.

PREP TIME: 5 minutes COOK TIME: 30–40 minutes
YIELD: 1 9×5×2.5-inch loaf

Pumpkin Yogurt Snack Cake

INGREDIENTS

1 cup dark brown sugar
½ cup butter, melted
½ cup Greek yogurt
½ cup pumpkin puree
½ cup granulated sugar
2 eggs
1 tablespoon orange zest
1 teaspoon vanilla extract
2¼ cups all-purpose flour, spooned and leveled
½ cup chopped, toasted walnuts
3 teaspoons baking powder
1 teaspoon kosher salt
1 teaspoon pumpkin pie spice
½ teaspoon baking soda

DIRECTIONS

Preheat the oven to 350°. Butter and flour a loaf pan or 9-inch cake pan.

Whisk the first 8 ingredients together, then gently fold in the dry ingredients. Do not overmix. Pour into prepared pan, and bake for 30 to 40 minutes.

Englevale, North Dakota. Baby Grandma Gloria and her cousin, Bud.

PREP TIME: 5 minutes YIELD: 15–20 pieces of toast

Cinnamon and Sugar Toasts

> There were six of us kids growing up, including cousins, at any one time in our home. A toaster sometimes just wouldn't do the job for all those little mouths. My mom would put buttered bread on a broiler pan with the cinnamon and sugar mixture on top and pop it under the broiler for a few minutes. It was a fast way to get a lot of toast done. I generally make 4 to 6 slices at a time, with plenty of spiced sugar to store for next time.

CINNAMON SUGAR

½ cup sugar

1 teaspoon spice, like ground cinnamon or pumpkin pie spice

½ teaspoon kosher salt

Butter and bread

DIRECTIONS

Set broiler to high, then simply spread a generous helping of butter onto the bread of your choice. We use a country buttermilk loaf. Mix sugar, spice, and salt in a small bowl. Sprinkle each slice with 1 teaspoon of spiced sugar, and broil for 1 to 3 minutes to bubble and brown.

Gresham, Oregon. Great-Auntie Carol and Great-Aunt Jerry.

SWEETS 197

PREP TIME: 10 minutes COOK TIME: 25–30 minutes
YIELD: 1 9×13-inch pan

Peanut Butter and Jam Cookie Bars

INGREDIENTS

½ cup butter, softened

1 cup peanut butter

1 cup dark brown sugar

½ cup granulated sugar

1 teaspoon vanilla extract

2 eggs

1½ cups all-purpose flour

1 teaspoon baking powder

1 teaspoon salt

1–1½ cups prepared jam (we use strawberry)

DIRECTIONS

Preheat the oven to 350°. Cream the butter, peanut butter, sugars, and vanilla together by hand or with a stand mixer; add the eggs, and mix together. Gently fold in the flour, baking powder, and salt.

Press half the dough into a parchment-lined 9-by-13-inch pan. Spread jam over top of the dough. Dot the surface with the other half of the dough.

Bake for 25 to 30 minutes until golden brown but still gooey. Be careful not to overbake.

PREP TIME: 20 minutes YIELD: 5 apples

Salted Caramel Apples

When I think of fall, I definitely think of caramel. I also think of being a chubby kid, toting a pillowcase around our wet and cold neighborhood, dreading the scary houses, and wanting only the good candy. Inevitably, there were houses giving out gross stuff and waxy chocolate pumpkins, but there were a few houses giving out the goods: real peanut butter cups or actual Skittles. I have never been a Halloween girl, but when October rolls around, I do think of a perfect caramel apple: a buttery, salty, and gooey treat wrapped around a juicy, tart apple. I wanted to try my hand at a fresh caramel apple. We tested so many recipes, and I've got to be really honest: homemade caramel is wonderful for candy and individual butter caramels, but in a blind test, the individually wrapped caramels won out each time, simply for their sticking ability! Everything homemade slid right off the apples; I even used sandpaper to rough 'em up. (The things you'll try while styling a photograph.) The wrapped, premade caramel is stable and takes on flavors perfectly. I added heavy whipping cream, flaky sea salt, and a touch of hazelnut liquor for the adult apples. We also thought, *Hey, who needs Popsicle sticks when you can use an apple branch?* These guys are perfect for girls' nights, date nights, or crafts with the kiddos. Move over pumpkin carving; branchy caramel apples are in town!

INGREDIENTS

20–25 individually wrapped butter caramels, like Kraft

¼ cup heavy whipping cream

5–6 organic or farm-fresh apples (no wax)

5–6 cleaned, trimmed 8-inch-long branches

1–2 tablespoons hazelnut liqueur

Sea salt to taste

DIRECTIONS

Melt the caramels and cream in a heavy-bottomed saucepan over medium heat. Watch this carefully, but while it's melting, prepare the apples. Use a paring knife to slice an X that is at least 1 inch deep at the top of each apple. Carefully shove the branches into the Xs, creating a sturdy handle to dunk and hold the apple with.

Remove the melted caramel from the heat, and add the sea salt and liqueur if you'd like. Gently dunk the apples into the melted caramel and, using a spoon, drag the caramel up the sides to coat. Lift above the caramel to let excess drip off, and repeat for a thicker shell. Place the finished apples onto parchment squares to cure for at least an hour. Sprinkle with extra-flaky salt before caramel sets.

PREP TIME: 10 minutes COOK TIME: 30–35 minutes
YIELD: 1 9×13-inch cake or 2 8- or 9-inch round cakes

Weeknight Yellow Cake with Fudge Frosting

Who eats cake on a weeknight? Growing up, we made yellow cake from a box all the time. My mother would allow any of us to mix it up and bake it and spread a can of frosting on top. There didn't have to be any special occasion. I am reminded of the ways God blesses us when I make a just-because, out-of-the-blue special treat. God does this for his beloved ones on the regular. No expectations, just a big ole *Hey, I love you. You are doing great.* We all need that. I try to cut back on sugar these days, but every once in a while, for no good reason other than we are alive so let's celebrate, Noah will find a yellow cake when he comes home from school. It says *Hey, I love you, buddy, and you are doing great.* No expectations—just enjoy it after dinner and maybe a little slice for breakfast.

INGREDIENTS

½ cup butter, softened

2 cups granulated sugar

1 teaspoon vanilla extract

1 teaspoon kosher salt

3 eggs

¼ cup mild oil, suitable for baking

½ cup heavy whipping cream

2¼ cups all-purpose flour, spooned and leveled

1 tablespoon baking powder

FUDGE FROSTING

3 cups confectioners' sugar

1 cup butter, softened

½ cup hot fudge, at room temp (store bought is just fine)

1 teaspoon kosher salt

DIRECTIONS

Preheat the oven to 350°. Cream butter, sugar, vanilla, and salt until light and fluffy, making sure to scrape down the sides of the bowl. Add eggs to the bowl one at a time, beating after each addition. Add oil to the bowl, and beat until the batter becomes smooth. Scrape down the sides of the bowl. Slowly add whipping cream as the mixer is running.

While this beats for 3 minutes, whisk the flour and baking powder in a separate bowl.

Fold the flour into the batter in three parts. Mix only until it's all incorporated.

Pour into two 8- or 9-inch cake pans or a 9-by-13-inch baking pan. Bake for 30 to 35 minutes or until a pick comes out clean.

While the cake cools, mix all the ingredients for the Fudge Frosting. Frost the cooled cake, and enjoy after dinner any old night of the week.

PREP TIME: 10 minutes COOK TIME: 12–14 minutes
YIELD: 6–8 scones

Spiced Pumpkin Scones with Spiced Cream Icing

SCONES

2 cups all-purpose flour

1 cup sugar

2 teaspoons baking powder

1 teaspoon pumpkin pie spice

1 teaspoon kosher salt

½ teaspoon baking soda

½ cup canned pumpkin puree

½ cup heavy cream

½ cup plus 2 tablespoons cold butter

ICING

1 cup confectioners' sugar

¼ cup heavy cream

¼ teaspoon pumpkin pie spice

1 pinch salt

DIRECTIONS

Line a baking sheet with parchment paper; set aside. Whisk all the dry ingredients thoroughly in a large mixing bowl. Whisk the pumpkin puree and heavy cream together in a separate bowl.

Add the cold butter to the flour and mix, using a pastry cutter or fork, until it's nice and crumbly, the size of peas. Make a well in the center of the flour mixture, and pour the pumpkin cream in. Gently mix until it just comes together. This dough is on the moist side.

Turn the dough out onto a floured surface, and make an 8-to-10-inch disk no more than 2 inches thick. Place the disk on a baking sheet, and put it in the freezer while you preheat the oven to 375°.

Remove the scone dough from the freezer. Slice it in half, then into quarters. Then cut each quarter in half again to yield 8 scones.

Bake for 12 to 14 minutes or until scones are puffed and lightly golden brown. Cool before icing.

FOR THE ICING

Mix all the ingredients until smooth; spoon over cooled scones.

SWEETS 203

PREP TIME: 10 minutes COOK TIME: 12–14 minutes, inactive 30 minutes to overnight YIELD: 2 dozen

Vanilla Bean Sugar Cookies

Forty-four years have come and gone since my father, fresh out of high school, left family and friends to join the army. His grandma Mac, a constant in his life, would make him Christmas cookies and mail them every year for his birthday on December 16 to wherever in the world he was stationed. My dad looked forward to that shoebox stuffed with cookies, often broken, sometimes weeks old (if they had traveled overseas). Those cookies meant more to him than any gift ever could. That shoebox from that Scottish woman meant he was loved; they meant that somewhere, no matter what, she was thinking of him. It was a piece of his home that he could cherish. She sent cookies to my dad up until she passed away. This year, I'm making my dad a shoebox of cookies. I thought long and hard about what to get the greatest man I've ever known. He came from nothing and has given me so much. Everyone has a gift guide, and we're bombarded with all the tricky new stuff we can buy for one another. But what if the ultimate goal this Christmas was to show love?

Betty Crocker might have written an iconic sugar-cookie recipe back in the fifties, but I have perfected it by using real butter, farm-fresh eggs, and a healthy dose of real vanilla beans. Christmas cookies are sacred in our home for all they represent. I can remember spreading tin foil over our entire kitchen table and baking quadruple batches when I was growing up. They would always have messy, pastel cream cheese icing and needed an overnight open-air cure to make sure the cookies were cakey and not crisp before being stored. No one wants a crispy sugar cookie. Sugar cookies mean far more than jingle bells and twinkly lights. I feel like the simple sugar cookie is a gesture of goodwill. I don't know of any family that doesn't share a cookie around the holidays. These are the cookies to end the year on a hopeful note, reflecting on all that's happened and looking forward to what is to come.

Great-Grandma Mac.

SWEETS 205

CONTINUED

Vanilla Bean Sugar Cookies

SUGAR COOKIE DOUGH

1 cup butter, softened

2 tablespoons cream cheese, softened

1½ cups confectioners' sugar

1 egg

Seeds scraped from 1 vanilla bean

1 teaspoon salt

1 teaspoon almond extract

2½ cups all-purpose flour

1 teaspoon cream of tartar

CREAM CHEESE FROSTING

1 cup butter, softened

1 teaspoon almond extract

1 pinch salt

8 ounces cream cheese, softened

4–6 cups confectioners' sugar

DIRECTIONS

Preheat the oven to 350°. Cream the butter, cream cheese, and sugar together in a large mixing bowl until light and fluffy, about 3 minutes; add the egg, vanilla, salt, and almond extract; mix well. Add the flour and cream of tartar, and mix by hand until it just comes together. Refrigerate dough for at least 30 minutes, but overnight is best.

When you are ready to bake, line 2 cookie sheets with parchment paper. Roll the dough into a ¼-inch-thick rough circle, and use your favorite cookie cutter to cut out shapes; place them on baking sheet. Bake for 12 to 14 minutes until set.

Continue this process until you've used up all the dough. Cool cookies on sheets of foil, and frost once completely cool. These cookies are fine to eat right away, but I think they get their signature touch frosted and left out overnight. We don't put them away until the next morning.

FOR THE FROSTING

Simply cream the butter, almond extract, salt, and cream cheese until light and fluffy; slowly add the confectioners' sugar. I like mine less sweet, so we do 4 cups of confectioners' sugar, but you can use up to 6 cups. Feel free to color small bowls of the frosting, and decorate cookies with sprinkles or tiny candies.

CONTINUED

Vanilla Bean Sugar Cookies

CHRISTMAS COOKIE PRO TIPS

- Double, or even triple, the dough, and freeze it in disks to pull out all season.
- Keep a little well of flour to rest cookie cutters in before and after cutting to ensure a clean cut.
- Bake cookies only in the top two racks of the oven to prevent an overcooked bottom.
- Skip the frosting, and mix in dried fruit, chocolate, coconut, or nuts.

SWEETS

PREP TIME: 10 minutes COOK TIME: 25–30 minutes
YIELD: 1 9×9-inch or 10×10-inch baking dish

Sticky Toffee Pudding

Frozen nights and early evenings call for a revamped classic. The self-saucing pudding is quite the rage in Great Britain, and I think for good cause: tender cake with the perfect amount of goo at the bottom! I am a huge fan of even more butterscotch goodness, so we opted for a pouring toffee sauce as well. Add a creamy scoop of vanilla ice cream, and you've got a spiced, warm dessert that rivals all others—and might remind you of your grandma in the best way possible. Your perfect winter treat—so easy, you can enjoy it midweek!

INGREDIENTS

1 cup pitted dried dates

½ cup unsweetened apple juice

½ cup plus 3 tablespoons butter, softened and divided

2 cups dark brown sugar, divided

3 eggs

1 teaspoon salt

1 teaspoon vanilla extract

1 teaspoon pumpkin pie spice

½ teaspoon cinnamon

1¼ cup all-purpose flour

1 teaspoon baking powder

1 teaspoon baking soda

1 cup boiling water

Heavy cream for garnish

EXTRA TOFFEE SAUCE

¾ cup heavy cream

1 cup dark brown sugar

1 pinch salt

DIRECTIONS

Preheat the oven to 350°. Generously butter a 9-by-9-inch or 10-by-10-inch baking dish; set aside. Bring the dates and apple juice to a boil, carefully smashing with a fork; cover and remove from heat. Meanwhile, cream ½ cup butter and 1 cup dark brown sugar until light and fluffy; add the eggs one at a time, and mix until well incorporated. Add the salt, vanilla, and spices. Fold in the flour, baking powder, and baking soda until just mixed. Add the hot date mixture with the mixer running on low.

Spoon the cake batter into a baking dish. Dot the top of the cake with the remaining soft butter, and sprinkle the remaining 1 cup dark brown sugar over that. Pour the boiling water over the top of the cake (I use the dirty date pan to bring water to a boil), and bake for 25 to 30 minutes or until the cake has set and the top has crackled slightly. Allow to cool for at least 10 minutes before scooping to serve.

FOR THE TOFFEE SAUCE

Simply cook the cream and sugar together over medium heat until sugar dissolves, about 3 to 4 minutes, and add salt. To serve, spoon out the heavenly pudding, and drizzle a bit of sauce and heavy cream over the top. Serve with vanilla ice cream or by itself. It's something your family will enjoy for years to come.

PREP TIME: 5 minutes COOK TIME: 25–30 minutes
YIELD: 1 9×13-inch sheet cake or 2 8-inch round cakes

White Cake with Raspberry Jam and Coconut

When I was turning six years old, my mom told me to invite all the church girls over and have a party. I remember opening an envelope of pennies from my best friend, Lacy. I had no idea that my mom, who had four kids by this time, had made me a white cake with raspberry jam and a big 6 made of coconut. The top layer of the cake slid off to the floor. She cried and was so upset. All I remember to this day is how delicious that cake was and how special I felt with my envelope of pennies. Don't worry too much about disappointing your children. You are their hero. I still love white cake and coconut.

INGREDIENTS

½ cup butter, softened

2 cups sugar

1 teaspoon vanilla extract

1 teaspoon kosher salt

4 egg whites, divided

¼ cup mild oil, suitable for baking

½ cup heavy whipping cream

2¼ cups all-purpose flour, spooned and leveled

1 tablespoon baking powder

Coconut, jam, and whipped cream for garnish (melted chocolate is also lovely)

DIRECTIONS

Preheat the oven to 350°. Cream the butter, sugar, vanilla, and salt until light and fluffy, making sure to scrape down the sides of the bowl. Add the egg whites to the bowl one at a time, beating after each addition. Add the oil, and beat until the batter becomes smooth. Scrape down the sides of the bowl. Slowly add the whipping cream as the mixer is running.

While this beats for 3 minutes, whisk the flour and baking powder in a separate bowl. Fold the flour into the batter in three parts. Mix only until it's just incorporated.

Pour into two 8-inch or 9-inch cake pans or a 9-by-13-inch baking dish. Bake for 25 to 30 minutes, or until a pick comes out clean. Remove from oven and cool completely.

CONTINUED

White Cake with Raspberry Jam and Coconut

RASPBERRY JAM

1 cup raspberry jam

1 cup fresh raspberries

3 tablespoons freshly squeezed orange juice

1 teaspoon orange zest

⅛ teaspoon salt

WHIPPED CREAM

2 cups heavy whipping cream

¼ cup confectioners' sugar

½ teaspoon vanilla extract

¼ teaspoon kosher salt

FOR THE JAM

Warm all the ingredients in a medium saucepan over medium heat until the fresh raspberries just begin to fall apart and the prepared jam marries with the juice. Cool the jam completely before adding to the cake.

FOR THE WHIPPED CREAM

Whip all the ingredients in the bowl of a stand mixer or with a hand mixer until soft peaks form.

TO PREPARE THE CAKE FOR SERVICE

Simply spread the jam over the top of the cake and sprinkle the coconut over the jam. To serve, spoon a healthy scoop of the whipped cream alongside each slice of cake.

Me on my sixth birthday.

PREP TIME: 10 minutes COOK TIME: inactive 2 hours
YIELD: 6 1-cup ramekins

Dark Chocolate and Salted Caramel Panna Cotta

INGREDIENTS

6 cups heavy whipping cream

1 cup sugar

1 vanilla bean, split and scraped

½ cup cocoa powder

1 pinch sea salt

1½ packets plain gelatin

Toasted pistachios, for topping

SALTED CARAMEL

2 cups sugar

1 cup cream

2 tablespoons butter

1 teaspoon salt

DIRECTIONS

Bring the cream, sugar, vanilla bean, cocoa powder, and salt to a gentle simmer over medium-low heat. You want bubbles to appear around the rim of the pan; do not boil.

While the cream is simmering, bloom the gelatin in 4 to 6 tablespoons of ice-cold water. Once the hot cream is ready, pour 1 cup of it into the gelatin to temper it, then add the mixture back to the rest of the cream and whisk for 2–3 minutes.

Remove the vanilla bean. Pour the cream into 1-cup ramekins. Refrigerate for 2 hours or up to overnight.

FOR THE CARAMEL

Melt the sugar in a heavy-bottomed saucepan over medium heat. Do not stir the sugar as it melts, but you may shake or swirl the pan to break up any clumps. Once the sugar is melted and bubbling, wait for a deep-amber color to appear; it might almost seem as if it's going to burn.

Moving quickly, remove from heat and add the cream; it will hiss and bubble, and you can stir it in at that point. Add the butter, and swirl the pan to melt it together. Add salt at the last minute, pour into a pint-sized jar, and cool completely. Caramel will last up to 3 weeks in the refrigerator.

SWEETS 213

PREP TIME: 10 minutes COOK TIME: 12 minutes, inactive 4 hours
YIELD: 1 10-inch pie plate

Lemon Chiffon Pie

CRUST

15 packaged shortbread cookies

3 tablespoons butter

½ teaspoon kosher salt

FILLING

1 envelope gelatin

4 tablespoons water

Juice and zest of 3 juicy lemons

2 cups sugar

3 eggs, plus 2 yolks

2 tablespoons butter

1 pinch salt

2 cups heavy whipping cream

DIRECTIONS

Preheat the oven to 350°. Crush the cookies, add the butter and salt, mix well, and press into a pie plate. Bake for 12 minutes. Cool completely before adding filling.

Create an ice bath by combining 3 cups ice and 3 cups water in a bowl significantly larger than the pot you are cooking the lemon mixture in. Bloom the gelatin in the water, and set aside.

Whisk the lemon juice, sugar, eggs, butter, and salt in a medium saucepan over medium heat until it's slightly thickened. Whisk constantly to keep the eggs from scrambling.

Whisk the gelatin into the hot mixture. Set the pan directly into the ice bath, and whisk to cool.

While this sits, whip cream. Once the lemon mixture is cooled, gently fold it into the whipped cream, and pour into the cooled pie crust. Refrigerate the pie for at least 4 hours before serving.

PREP TIME: 5 minutes **COOK TIME:** 45 minutes **YIELD:** 4–6 servings

Old-Fashioned Rice Pudding

INGREDIENTS

4 cups whole milk (see note)

3 cups cooked white rice

1 cup brown sugar

1 cup heavy cream

1 cinnamon stick

3–5 green cardamom pods

1 tablespoon butter

1 teaspoon vanilla extract (or
   1 vanilla bean, split and
   scraped)

1 teaspoon salt

½ teaspoon apple pie spice

½ cup golden raisins (optional)

1 tablespoon orange zest
   (optional)

DIRECTIONS

Combine all the ingredients in a large saucepan, and bring to a simmer over medium heat, then reduce to low. Stew uncovered, stirring continually, for 45 minutes. This yields a thick, luscious porridge.

Remove the large spices before serving. Finish with a splash of heavy cream, toasted nuts, or spiced stewed apples in each warm bowl, along with a sprinkle of cinnamon.

Note: Milk likes to boil over when it gets too hot; make sure you keep the heat low and remove it quickly if it gets too wild. If you start with overcooked or mushy rice, you will have a much more mushy porridge than if the rice has a bit more bite.

SWEETS 215

PREP TIME: 10 minutes **COOK TIME:** 30–40 minutes
YIELD: 1 9-inch galette

Strawberry Galette with Crème Fraîche

BUTTER PASTRY

2 cups all-purpose flour

1 cup butter

¼ cup sugar

1 teaspoon kosher salt

STRAWBERRY FILLING

3 cups sliced strawberries

¾ cup sugar

2 tablespoons all-purpose flour

1 teaspoon salt

Plain crème fraîche for garnish

DIRECTIONS

Preheat the oven to 350°. Place the flour, butter, sugar, and salt into a stand mixer. Mix until it begins to come together.

Turn the crumbles out onto a floured surface, and roll into a 12-inch disk. Gently fold over onto itself, and lay it on a parchment-lined baking sheet. Unfold it, and prepare the filling.

Mix the strawberries with the sugar, flour, and salt; pour into the center of the pastry, and fold the edges up onto itself. Bake for 30 to 40 minutes.

If you fancy a browned and glossy crust, brush an egg wash over the pastry edges, then sprinkle with sugar.

Fresh Blueberry and Chocolate Chip Cookies

PREP TIME: 5 minutes COOK TIME: 12–14 minutes
YIELD: 18–20 cookies

Fresh Blueberry and Chocolate Chip Cookies

INGREDIENTS

1 cup butter, softened

1 cup dark brown sugar

¾ cup granulated sugar

2 whole eggs

1 teaspoon vanilla extract

1 teaspoon kosher salt

2 cups all-purpose flour

1 teaspoon baking powder

¼ teaspoon baking soda

2 cups dark chocolate chips or chopped dark chocolate

1½ cups fresh blueberries

DIRECTIONS

Preheat the oven to 350°. Cream the butter and sugars; add the eggs one at a time, then add the vanilla extract and salt.

Fold in the flour, baking powder, and baking soda. Gently fold the chocolate and blueberries into the batter. Do not overmix.

Scoop 1-tablespoon dollops onto a parchment-lined baking sheet, and bake for 12 to 14 minutes.

PREP TIME: 15 minutes COOK TIME: 30–40 minutes, 30 minutes inactive YIELD: 1 9-inch galette

Apricot and Almond Shortbread Galette

"Hey, Mama. I played hide the peach with you." Tiny smirk and hands folded behind his back.

"What do you mean, 'hide the peach,' Noah?" I ask, blow-dryer in hand as I feverishly try to get ready for an event.

"I mean, I took all your peaches and hid them all over your room."

I pause in disbelief, but slowly, laughter wells from within, and while I am mildly irritated, I can't help but stop what I am doing and follow my four-year-old all over my room as he says, "You're getting hotter...nope, colder," and we start to find all the tiny fruits (apricots, actually, not peaches) smashed into candleholders and under hats and in piles of laundry. I know this spells trouble—the kind of trouble you smell weeks later, with a few fruit flies buzzing around the one we didn't find. At this point, Noah had a few apricots in his hands and was taking bites out of all of them. After the game, the apricots were certainly worse for wear. I can only laugh during these times. I wasn't upset; it led me to make an apricot galette with all my mushy, bruised, but well-loved apricots. Now I don't think I'll ever be able to look at an apricot without remembering "hide the peach" while his tiny face lit up, and I stopped what I was doing to find them (to narrowly avoid disaster), but also just to be together. Life can wait. Your children are small for only a short time. Make all the pies, in whatever form you possibly can.

North Dakota. Auntie Edna, Great-Gran Thora, and Auntie Marge.

220 SWEETS

CONTINUED

Apricot and Almond Shortbread Galette

APRICOT FILLING

10–12 apricots, halved

1 cup brown sugar

2 tablespoons all-purpose flour

2 tablespoons butter

1 tablespoon lemon juice

1 teaspoon kosher salt

SHORTBREAD CRUST

2 cups all-purpose flour

1 cup butter, softened

¼ cup sliced almonds

½ cup sugar

½ teaspoon kosher salt

DIRECTIONS

Preheat the oven to 350°. Gently mix all the apricot filling ingredients together in a large mixing bowl, and set aside.

Put all the crust ingredients in the bowl of your stand mixer and mix until a loose ball of dough forms.

Press the dough together to form an 8-inch disk and refrigerate for 30 minutes. Remove from the fridge for 15 minutes before rolling into a large 12-to-14-inch disk on a floured surface.

Line a baking sheet with parchment paper, leaving a 1-inch rim. Gently place the disk of dough onto the lined pan. This dough is a bit crumbly, but that's okay. If it begins to tear or fall apart, just press it back together.

Pour the filling into the center, making sure 2 inches are free around the edges. Fold that 2-inch edge of dough up over the fruit and press and hold together.

Bake for 30 to 40 minutes or until golden and bubbly.

SWEETS 221

PREP TIME: 10 minutes **COOK TIME:** 25–30 minutes
YIELD: 1 10-inch tart

Pear and Almond Cream Tart

SHORTBREAD CRUST

2 cups all-purpose flour

1 cup butter, softened

¼ cup sugar

½ teaspoon salt

FILLING

2 cups almond flour

4 eggs

1 cup sugar

½ cup heavy cream

1 teaspoon salt

1 teaspoon vanilla extract

3 small pears

¼ cup brown sugar

DIRECTIONS

Preheat the oven to 350°. Add the crust ingredients to a stand mixer, and mix until crumbly (by hand works great as well). Press the crust into a 10-inch tart pan, and bake for 15 minutes.

For the filling, mix everything but the pears and brown sugar. Pour the almond cream into the warm crust. Slice the ripe pears in half, and use a small spoon or melon baller to remove the cores. Place the pear halves sliced-side up into the tart. Sprinkle the pears with the brown sugar. Bake for 25 to 30 minutes or until the cream filling has puffed around the pears and the tart top is golden brown.

222 SWEETS

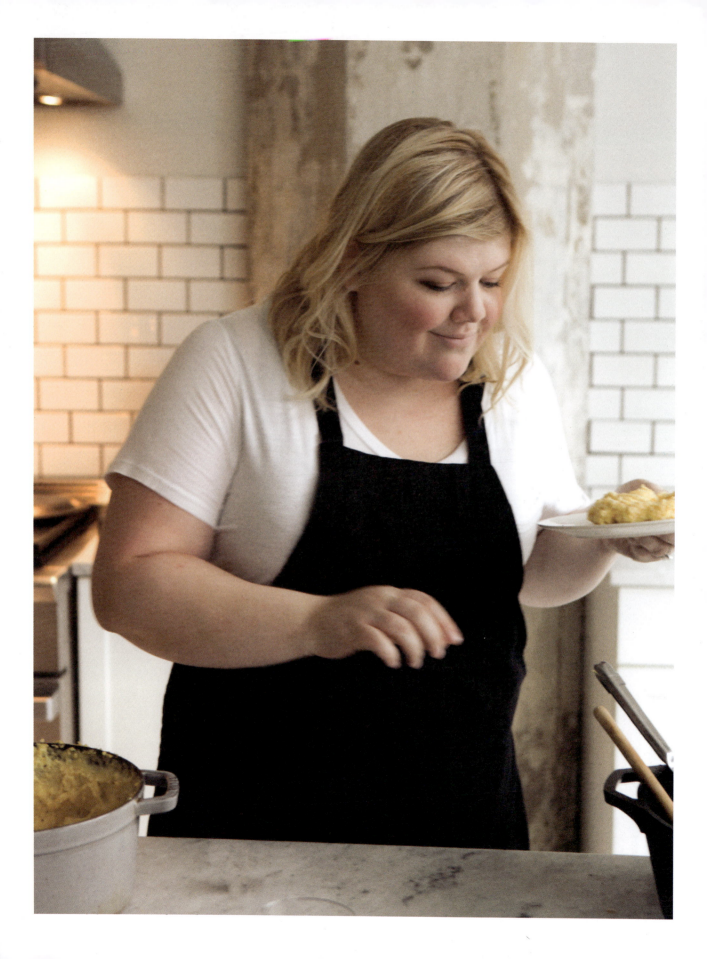

Closing Thoughts

It was our first Valentine's Day as a married couple. It was back during our restaurant days, and I'd probably put in a sixteen-hour day. I was grumpy and tired and had been picking on Mike, I'm sure. He didn't get me a card or chocolates, and it was the end of the day. I mumbled and grumbled and thought, *Gosh, how unthoughtful of him!*

I walked out to my car around midnight, after the ovens were scrubbed, and my feet just ached. I hit my key fob to unlock the car with real tears in my eyes from feeling unloved. My dome light came on, and through the dark, I could see something inside my car. I couldn't quite make it out, but I got nervous as I took a few steps forward. I could see flowers. A huge sense of relief washed over me as I opened the driver-side door to find dozens of roses and my very first enamel-covered Dutch oven. It was bright red and pink, and ivory roses were everywhere. A card on top said thank you. Imagine that: a thank-you card on Valentine's Day, for me, the grumpy brat who didn't always get things her way.

I thought I had wanted a silly box of chocolates when I woke up; instead, my dreams came true that evening. I just had to wait a bit longer.

Sometimes, waiting is exactly what we need. What are you waiting for these days? What are you hoping for? I want to encourage you that God knows all those desires and dreams in your heart. They will come to pass in His time. I promise that, no matter how long it takes, you will get there.

I am happy to say I've done some growing in the last few years, and my desires sure aren't what they used to be. I used to long for money and success. I can't say it enough now: God has shown me that true success is won in the heart. It's not about the things you amass, but more about the way you love and how much you give away.

My hope is that this book becomes an impetus for love and giving, a motivator to be with people. Know that the legacy you leave on this earth can be far sweeter than a posh career. To love your family well—to sit a spell and enjoy others' company—is the greatest treasure out there. Don't let your eyes fill with tears over the worldly things you don't possess; let your heart fill with joy over what you have.

I will forever be grateful for my tiny kitchen, with poor lighting and a coil-top range that isn't the prettiest. It's not what you have that's special; it's how you use it. In every book I write, I will close with this: I hope the recipes living in these pages become your own. I hope they feed your soul and nourish your heart. I hope the binding breaks, and you scribble in your changes.

My hope is that this book brings life for generations to come.

Index

Note: Page numbers in *italic* refer to photographs.

A

Aioli, Lemon Dill, 129
apples
   Apple Butterscotch Syrup, 143
   Apple Cider Pork Shoulder with Thyme and Sauerkraut, 30
   Cider Champagne Cocktail, 163
   Salted Caramel Apples, 200, *201*
   Spiced Stewed Apples, 179
   Yogurt Bowls with Stewed Apples, *154, 155*
Applesauce Bundt Cake, Grandma Hawkins's, 176, *177*
Apricot and Almond Shortbread Galette, 220–221
Asparagus, Garlic and Brown Butter, 90
author's personal story, xvii–xxiii

B

Bacon and White Bean Soup, *56*, 57

bars

Coconut Cream Lemon Bars, *184*, 185

Peanut Butter and Jam Cookie Bars, *198*, 199

BBQ Chicken Wings, Oven-Baked, 7

BBQ Sauce, Creamy, 24

Bean and Bacon Soup, White, *56*, 57

beef

Classic Oven-Braised Beef and Tomato Stew over Cream Cheese Polenta, *62*, 63

Hamburger Soup, 58

Homestyle Meatloaf Sandwich, *28*, 29

My Mom's Swiss Steak, 20

Puff Pastry Roast Beef Pot Pie, 17

Shepherd's Pie, 35

Sloppy Joes, 44, *45*

Swedish-Style Meatballs in Mushroom Cream Sauce, *32*, 33

Wine-and-Tomato-Braised Short Ribs over Parmesan Cauliflower Mash, *18*, 19

beverages, 159–169

blueberries

Blueberry Brown Sugar Baked French Toast Topped with Toasted Pecans, Buttermilk Maple Syrup, and Whipped Cream, 138–139

Fresh Blueberry and Chocolate Chip Cookies, *218*, 219

Bouillabaisse or Fish Stew, *60*, 61

Breadcrumb Topping, Buttery, 37

breakfast, 133–157

Brie and Tomatoes, Caramelized, *130*, 131

Broccoli and Cauliflower, Jenny's Perfectly Steamed, 110

Brownies, Cream Cheese, 178

Buttermilk Maple Syrup, 139

Buttermilk Ranch Dipping Sauce, 104

butternut squash. *See* squash

C

cakes

Aunt Libby's Carrot Cake, *172*, 173

Cherry Chip Cake with Cream Cheese Icing, 174

Chocolate Buttermilk Birthday Cake with Malted Chocolate Cream Cheese Frosting, 175

Coconut Bundt Cake with Lemon Curd, Toasted Coconut, and Soft Whipped Cream, *182*, *183*

Grandma Hawkins's Applesauce Bundt Cake, 176, *177*

Honey Butter Biscuit Strawberry Shortcake, *186*, 187–189

Mug Cakes, a.k.a. the Emotional Support Treat, *190*, 191

Pumpkin Yogurt Snack Cake, 196

Weeknight Yellow Cake with Fudge Frosting, 202

White Cake with Raspberry Jam and Coconut, 210–211

carrots

Aunt Libby's Carrot Cake, *172*, 173

Curried Carrot Soup, 66, 67–68

Roasted Carrots with Cilantro Yogurt, *88*, 89

Sheet-Pan Chicken and Carrots, 43

cauliflower

  Jenny's Perfectly Steamed Broccoli
    and Cauliflower, 110

  Mustard Chicken Thighs and Cauliflower, 21

  Parmesan Cauliflower Mash, 19

  Roasted Cauliflower and Capers, 95

Celeriac Root, Potato, and Parsnip Vegetable
  Soup, 64, *65*

Champagne Cocktail, Cider, 163

cheese

  Caramelized Brie and Tomatoes, *130*, 131

  Toasted Pimento Cheese Sandwiches, 42

  White Cheddar Toast with Dill
    and Tomatoes, *120*, 121

cherries

  Cherry Chip Cake with Cream Cheese Icing, 174

  Dark Chocolate and Cherry Cream
    Cheese Whoopie Pies, *180*, 181

  Pineapple and Cherry Crumble, 194

chicken. *See* poultry

Chiles Rellenos, Baked, 156

chocolate

  Chocolate Buttermilk Birthday Cake with Malted
    Chocolate Cream Cheese Frosting, 175

  Chocolate Chip and Rye Pancakes, 149

  Cream Cheese Brownies, 178

  Dark Chocolate and Cherry Cream
    Cheese Whoopie Pies, *180*, 181

  Dark Chocolate and Salted Caramel
    Panna Cotta, *212*, 213

  Fresh Blueberry and Chocolate
    Chip Cookies, *218*, 219

  Hot Chocolate, *162*, 163

  Weeknight Yellow Cake with Fudge Frosting, 202

Chowder Bread Bowls, Classic New England
  Clam, *70*, 71

Cider Champagne Cocktail, 163

Cilantro Yogurt, 89

Cinnamon and Sugar Toasts, 197

Citronette-Dressed Greens, Seared Salmon with,
  25

Citrus Vinaigrette, Classic, 103

clams

  Bouillabaisse or Fish Stew, *60*, 61

  Buttermilk Fried Oysters and
    Razor Clams, *128*, 129

  Classic New England Clam Chowder
    Bread Bowls, *70*, 71

Coconut Bundt Cake with Lemon Curd, Toasted
  Coconut, and Soft Whipped Cream, 182, *183*

Coconut Cream Lemon Bars, *184*, 185

Coffee, Egg, 167

condiments. *See* sauces and toppings

cookies

  Christmas Cookie Pro Tips, 207

  Dark Chocolate and Cherry Cream
    Cheese Whoopie Pies, *180*, 181

  Fresh Blueberry and Chocolate
    Chip Cookies, *218*, 219

  Peanut Butter and Jam Cookie Bars, *198*, 199

  Vanilla Bean Sugar Cookies, *204*, 205–207

Corn with Chipotle and Feta, Off-the-Cob
  Street, *96*, 97

Cornbread and Maple Syrup, Fluffy, *146*, 147

crab

Fresh Crab Feast, 40

Kale and Fresh Crab Caesar Salad with
Pepita Caesar Dressing, 98, 99

Cream Cheese and Honey Fruit Dip, 194

Cream Cheese Schmear, 144

Cream of Wheat, 157

Crème Fraîche, Strawberry Galette with, 216,
217

Crème Fraîche Whipped Cream, 189

Croutons, Herbed, 98

Crumble, Pineapple and Cherry, 194

Crust, Shortbread, 195, 221, 222

cucumbers

Pickles, *124*, 125

Tomato and Cucumber Salad, 106

Curried Carrot Soup, 66, 67–68

Curried Halibut, *8*, 9

Curry Soup with Grilled Chicken Skewers, Thai
Green, 76, 77

D

desserts, 171–223

drinks, 159–169

E

eggs

Baked Chiles Rellenos, 156

Bus-Stop Egg Sandwiches, *150*, 151–152

Caramelized Onion Frittata, *140*, 141

Egg Coffee, 167

Soft Scrambled Eggs, 148

Sweet Potato Hash and Fried Eggs, 142

F

fish

Bouillabaisse or Fish Stew, *60*, 61

Curried Halibut, *8*, 9

Seared Salmon with Citronette-Dressed Greens, *25*

Ultimate Classic Beer-Battered Fish
and Chips, The, *14*, 15–16

French Toast, Blueberry Brown Sugar Baked,
Topped with Toasted Pecans, Buttermilk
Maple Syrup, and Whipped Cream, 138–139

fries

Homestyle Garlic Fries, *122*, 123

Spicy Sweet Potato Fries with Sun-
Dried Tomato Mayo, 127

Ultimate Classic Beer-Battered Fish
and Chips, The, *14*, 15–16

Frittata, Caramelized Onion, *140*, 141

Fruit Dip, Cream Cheese and Honey, 194

G

galettes
    Apricot and Almond Shortbread Galette, 220–221
    Strawberry Galette with Crème Fraîche, 216, *217*
Grapefruit Paloma, 161
gravies
    Cafeteria Chicken Gravy, 10–11
    Smothered Chicken and Mushroom Gravy, 38–39
    Turkey Gravy, 34

H

Hamburger Soup, 58
Hash and Fried Eggs, Sweet Potato, 142
Herbed Croutons, 98
Herby Peas, *82*, 83
Honey Mustard Sauce, 24
Hot Chocolate, *162*, 163

I

Italian Sodas, 164–166, *165*

K

Kale and Fresh Crab Caesar Salad with Pepita
    Caesar Dressing, 98, *99*
Ketchup, Spicy, 16

L

Lemon Bars, Coconut Cream, *184*, 185
Lemon Chiffon Pie, 214
Lemon Dill Aioli, 129
Lemonade, Old-Fashioned, *160*, 161

M

Mac 'n' Cheese, Stovetop, *36*, 37
main dishes, 1–53
Marinara, Fresh, 49
Mash, Parmesan Cauliflower, 19
Mayo, Sun-Dried Tomato, 127
measurements, xxv–xxvi
Meatballs in Mushroom Cream Sauce, Swedish-
    Style, *32*, 33
Meatloaf Sandwich, Homestyle, *28*, 29
Mojito Floats, 168, *169*
Mug Cakes, a.k.a. the Emotional Support Treat,
    190, 191
Mushroom Cream Sauce, Swedish-Style
    Meatballs in, *32*, 33

Mushroom Gravy, Smothered Chicken and, 38–39

Mustard Chicken Thighs and Cauliflower, 21

Mustard-Roasted Chicken and Potatoes, 46

O

onions

Caramelized Onion Frittata, *140*, 141

Thora's Steakhouse Crispy Onion Rings with Buttermilk Ranch Dipping Sauce, 104, *105*

Oysters and Razor Clams, Buttermilk Fried, *128*, 129

P

Paloma, Grapefruit, 161

pancakes

Buttermilk Pumpkin Pancakes with Toasted Pecans and Cream Cheese Schmear, 144, *145*

Chocolate Chip and Rye Pancakes, 149

Cinnamon Vanilla Ricotta Pancakes, 136, *137*

Panna Cotta, Dark Chocolate and Salted Caramel, *212*, 213

Parsnip, Potato, and Celeriac Root Vegetable Soup, 64, *65*

pasta

Angel Hair Pasta in Tomato Cream, 31

Fresh Pasta with Tiger Shrimp and Cream, 6

Peas and Orzo, *100*, 101

Stovetop Mac 'n' Cheese, *36*, 37

Stuffed Shells, *4*, 5

Peanut Butter and Jam Cookie Bars, *198*, 199

Pear and Almond Cream Tart, 222, *223*

peas

Herby Peas, *82*, 83

Peas and Orzo, *100*, 101

Pepita Caesar Dressing, 98

Pickles, *124*, 125

pies

Dark Chocolate and Cherry Cream Cheese Whoopie Pies, *180*, 181

Lemon Chiffon Pie, 214

Shepherd's Pie, 35

Walnut Pie, 195

Pineapple and Cherry Crumble, 194

Pizza, Homemade Sheet-Pan, 26, *27*

polenta

Butternut Squash Polenta, 85

Classic Oven-Braised Beef and Tomato Stew over Cream Cheese Polenta, *62*, 63

Cream Cheese Polenta, 107

Popcorn, Rosemary and Parmesan, 126

Pork Shoulder with Thyme and Sauerkraut, Apple Cider, 30

Pot Pie, Puff Pastry Roast Beef, 17

potatoes

Aunty Pat's Dilly Potatoes, 86, *87*

Caramelized Onion Frittata, *140*, 141

Classic New England Clam Chowder Bread Bowls, *70*, 71

232 INDEX

Creamy Buttermilk and Parsley
Mashed Potatoes, 84
Easter Potatoes with Feta, Cream
Cheese, and Dill, 92–94, *93*
Homestyle Garlic Fries, *122*, 123
Mom's Scalloped Potatoes, 111
Mustard-Roasted Chicken and Potatoes, 46
Old-Fashioned Dill and Mustard
Potato Salad, *112*, 113
Potato, Parsnip, and Celeriac Root
Vegetable Soup, 64, *65*
Real Baked Potato Soup, *59*
Shepherd's Pie, 35
Spring Potatoes, 109
Ultimate Classic Beer-Battered Fish
and Chips, The, *14*, 15–16

poultry
Baked Chicken Parmesan, *48*, 49
Cafeteria Chicken Gravy, 10–11
Company Chicken, 47
Gloria's Oven-Fried Chicken Legs, 12, *13*
Mustard Chicken Thighs and Cauliflower, 21
Mustard-Roasted Chicken and Potatoes, 46
Old-School Cracker Crumb Nuggets
and Sauces, *22*, 23–24
Olive Chicken, *50*, 51–53
Oven-Baked BBQ Chicken Wings, 7
Perfect Chicken Stock, 69
Sheet-Pan Chicken and Carrots, 43
Smothered Chicken and Mushroom Gravy, 38–39
Stuffed Shells, *4*, 5
Swedish-Style Meatballs in Mushroom
Cream Sauce, *32*, 33

Taco Soup, 72, 73
Thai Green Curry Soup with Grilled
Chicken Skewers, 76, 77
Turkey Gravy, 34
Pudding, Old-Fashioned Rice, 215
Pudding, Sticky Toffee, 208, *209*
pumpkin
Buttermilk Pumpkin Pancakes with Toasted
Pecans and Cream Cheese Schmear, 144, *145*
Pumpkin Yogurt Snack Cake, 196
Spiced Pumpkin Scones with
Spiced Cream Icing, 203

R

Radishes, Roasted, *108*, 109
Ranch Dipping Sauce, Buttermilk, 104
Ranch Sauce, Sour Cream, 24
Rice Pudding, Old-Fashioned, 215

S

salads
Everyday Green Salad, *102*, 103
Kale and Fresh Crab Caesar Salad with
Pepita Caesar Dressing, 98, *99*
Seared Salmon with Citronette-Dressed Greens, 25
Tomato and Cucumber Salad, 106

INDEX 233

sandwiches
  Bus-Stop Egg Sandwiches, *150*, 151–152
  Homestyle Meatloaf Sandwich, *28*, 29
  Sloppy Joes, 44, *45*
  Toasted Pimento Cheese Sandwiches, 42
  White Cheddar Toast with Dill
    and Tomatoes, *120*, 121
sauces and toppings. *See also* gravies
  Apple Butterscotch Syrup, 143
  Buttermilk Maple Syrup, 139
  Buttermilk Ranch Dipping Sauce, 104
  Buttery Breadcrumb Topping, 37
  Cilantro Yogurt, 89
  Cream Cheese Schmear, 144
  Creamy BBQ Sauce, 24
  Crème Fraîche Whipped Cream, 189
  Fresh Marinara, 49
  Fresh Whipped Cream, 139
  Herbed Croutons, 98
  Honey Mustard Sauce, 24
  Lemon Dill Aioli, 129
  Sour Cream Ranch Sauce, 24
  Spicy Ketchup, 16
  Sun-Dried Tomato Mayo, 127
  Tartar Sauce, 16
  Thousand Island, 24
  Toffee Sauce, 208
Scones with Spiced Cream Icing, Spiced
  Pumpkin, 203
seafood
  Bouillabaisse or Fish Stew, *60*, 61
  Buttermilk Fried Oysters and
    Razor Clams, *128*, 129

  Classic New England Clam Chowder
    Bread Bowls, *70*, 71
  Curried Halibut, *8*, 9
  Fresh Crab Feast, 40
  Fresh Pasta with Tiger Shrimp and Cream, 6
  Garlic Butter Shrimp, 40, *41*
  Kale and Fresh Crab Caesar Salad with
    Pepita Caesar Dressing, 98, *99*
  Seared Salmon with Citronette-Dressed Greens, 25
  Ultimate Classic Beer-Battered Fish
    and Chips, The, *14*, 15–16
Shepherd's Pie, 35
Short Ribs over Parmesan Cauliflower Mash,
  Wine-and-Tomato-Braised, *18*, 19
Shortcake, Honey Butter Biscuit Strawberry,
  186, 187–189
shrimp
  Bouillabaisse or Fish Stew, *60*, 61
  Fresh Pasta with Tiger Shrimp and Cream, 6
  Garlic Butter Shrimp, 40, *41*
sides and vegetables, 79–115
Sloppy Joes, 44, *45*
snacks, 117–131
soups and stews, 55–77
Sour Cream Ranch Sauce, 24
Spinach, Creamed, 85
squash. *See also* pumpkin
  Butternut Squash Polenta, 85
  Molasses and Walnut Zucchini Bread, 192, *193*
  Roasted Butternut Squash with
    Parmesan Cheese, 91
Stock, Perfect Chicken, 69
strawberries

Honey Butter Biscuit Strawberry
    Shortcake, *186*, 187–189
Strawberry Galette with Crème Fraîche, 216, *217*
Stuffed Shells, *4, 5*
Sugar Cookies, Vanilla Bean, *204*, 205–207
Sun-Dried Tomato Mayo, 127
supper, 1–53
sweet potatoes
    Spicy Sweet Potato Fries with Sun-
        Dried Tomato Mayo, 127
    Sweet Potato Hash and Fried Eggs, 142
sweets, 171–223
syrups
    Apple Butterscotch Syrup, 143
    Buttermilk Maple Syrup, 139

Caramelized Brie and Tomatoes, *130*, 131
Fresh Marinara, 49
Roasted Tomato Soup, *74, 75*
Sun-Dried Tomato Mayo, 127
Tomato and Cucumber Salad, 106
White Cheddar Toast with Dill
    and Tomatoes, *120*, 121
Turkey Gravy, 34

T

Taco Soup, 72, *73*
Tart, Pear and Almond Cream, 222, *223*
Tartar Sauce, The Ultimate, 16
Thai Green Curry Soup with Grilled Chicken
    Skewers, 76, 77
Thousand Island, 24
Toast with Dill and Tomatoes, White Cheddar,
    120, 121
Toasted Pimento Cheese Sandwiches, 42
Toasts, Cinnamon and Sugar, 197
Toffee Pudding, Sticky, 208, *209*
tomatoes
    Angel Hair Pasta in Tomato Cream, 31

V

vegetables and sides, 79–115
Vegetables, Roasted Winter, 114, *115*
Vinaigrette, Classic Citrus, 103

W

Waffles with Apple Butterscotch Syrup, Whole-
    Grain, 143
Walnut Pie, 195
Whipped Cream, Crème Fraîche, 189
Whipped Cream, Fresh, 139
Whoopie Pies, Dark Chocolate and Cherry
    Cream Cheese, *180*, 181
Winter Vegetables, Roasted, 114, *115*

Y

yogurt
   Cilantro Yogurt, 89
   Pumpkin Yogurt Snack Cake, 196
   Yogurt Bowls with Stewed Apples, *154*, 155

Z

Zucchini Bread, Molasses and Walnut, 192, *193*

About the Author

Tacoma, Washington. Me.

Danielle Kartes

Danielle Kartes is an author and recipe developer living near Seattle, Washington, with her photographer husband, Michael, and their two sweet boys, Noah and Milo. Together, the Karteses run their boutique food, lifestyle, and commercial photography business, Rustic Joyful Food. Rustic Joyful Food promotes loving your life right where you are, no matter where you are at, and creating beautiful, delicious food that's fuss free with whatever you have available to you. Danielle is driven by happy accidents in the kitchen, her family, and her relationship with Jesus. Rustic Joyful Food's sophomore book, *Generations*, is a look at family comfort food and the heirloom recipes she was raised on. The pains of life are somehow healed in the kitchen, and it is the author's desire that you find something to love within these pages and truly make it your own.